LAURENCE WHISTLER

THE ENGLISH FESTIVALS

With a Foreword by James Russell

DEAN STREET PRESS

Published by Dean Street Press 2015

Copyright © 1947 Laurence Whistler

Foreword © 2015 James Russell

All Rights Reserved

Cover by DSP

First published in 1947 by William Heinemann Ltd

ISBN 978 1 910570 50 0

www.deanstreetpress.co.uk

FOR MY MOTHER

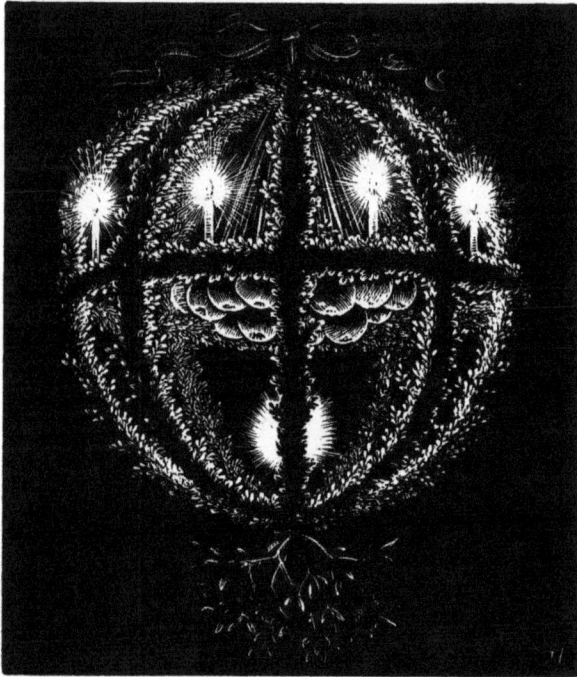

THE KISSING BOUGH OF ENGLISH CHRISTMAS.
Candles, evergreens and apples on a wire frame.
Wood engravings by Joan Hassall, showing the two forms of the device that preceded the Christmas tree in England. *See p. 44.*

LAURENCE WHISTLER
THE ENGLISH FESTIVALS

"His book has been written in delight and passes on delight to the reader... it has a lovely benevolence; the author's knowledge, his sense of values, his breadth of outlook are in evidence on every page." *John O'London's Weekly*

"There is scholarship here about the past, and delight in the festivals of today... a book that will be delightful to pick up again at any time of the year." *Sunday Times*

"Possessing enchantment of matter, it has also enchantment of manner." *Time and Tide*

"Its younger readers will find themselves educated, perhaps unconsciously, by publisher as well as author." *Observer*

"A charming book." *Country Life*

"A most charming and decorative volume." *Sunday Chronicle*

"Learning and common sense have gone to the making of this attractive, well-illustrated book." *Birmingham News*

"A delightful gift book for all the year round... altogether charming." *Edinburgh Evening News*

Also by Laurence Whistler

The Initials in the Heart

FOREWORD

BY

JAMES RUSSELL

This marvellous book is, at the most basic level, a guide to the traditional calendar customs of an old country, but delve into its elegantly written pages and you will discover much more. Laurence Whistler knew well the secular and religious history of England, but his approach to the subject was as much poetic as historical, intuitive as much as factual. The English Festivals were alive to him, and through them we get the sense that he felt a connection with rural and ecclesiastical culture stretching back a thousand years or more. This is not just a book about Christmas, Easter and the rest, but a celebration of a pagan, fun-loving England that we may still glimpse on May Day or Bonfire Night.

Written in the immediate aftermath of World War Two, *The English Festivals* combines the wit and wisdom of an old-fashioned Book of Days with the kind of personal opinion and hands-on instruction a 21st century writer might offer. The post-war perspective no doubt accounts in part for the nostalgic sense of innocent pleasures lost, but we should also remember that Whistler had recently lost his older brother Rex and his first wife Jill, both of whom died in 1944. Not that the book is in any sense gloomy. Rather the awareness of grief, both personal and general, lends gravitas to its central argument: that life in the here and now should be enjoyed.

Laurence Whistler was born in London in 1912 and studied at Oxford, where he enjoyed success as a poet, becoming the first recipient of the King's Gold Medal for Poetry in 1935. He also won the Chancellor's Essay Prize, and subsequently put his skills as prose writer to good use in the first significant biography of 18th century architect and writer Sir John Vanbrugh. Laurence and Rex shared a passion for early modern art and culture and, while the older brother put his knowledge to use creating splendid murals in a Romantic vein, the younger set about reviving the lost techniques of glass engraving.

Encouraged by Rex, Laurence taught himself the demanding art of point engraving on glass, mastering a stippling technique that allowed him to create delicate, atmospheric pictures, usually on blown glassware. His work evolved over the course of an extraordinary career, as he gradually shed the more rococo influence of his brother and focused instead on landscape, creating hauntingly beautiful works that really have to be seen to be fully appreciated. Likewise the numerous memorial pieces he made, not to mention the exquisitely engraved glass prism that stands in Salisbury Cathedral as a monument to Rex. How we experience these engravings depends greatly on the light, whether this is low winter sun shining obliquely on the engraved windows of Moreton Church, Dorset, or candlelight flickering on a blown glass bowl.

Whistler's fascination for light of all kinds flows through this book too, whether he is describing the transformation of Durham Cathedral into a 'lantern' during the celebration of Candlemas or advising parents to take their children out into the pre-dawn darkness of early summer so that they can experience the sunrise. Most poetic, and most personal, is his description of a family Christmas the centrepiece of which is a tree decorated with candles. 'Even to older eyes it seems to be more than it is, more than a conifer covered with objects of metal and glass and wax, this image of a tree whose buds are flames, flowering at midwinter...

'At a slight draught from the window,' he continues, 'the candles flow one way together, with a glance whose transcendental drift we are never quite in time to gather. Presently a twig, too near a flame, cracks in the heat, shrivels to the foot of a bird, and utters its one cry of fragrance.'

He is not talking here about the distant past, but about his own life. In 1939 he married Jill Furse, an actress who played significant roles in films such as *Goodbye, Mr Chips*, and with her he had two children, Simon and Caroline – known as Robin. Although Jill died soon after her daughter's birth, she and Laurence had already explored the traditions of Christmas and other festivals, and Robin remembers having a Christmas tree and a Kissing Bough every year, both illuminated by candles.

'Traditionally,' she recalls, 'the Kissing Bough was always made during the King's College carol service. I can't listen to that these days without expecting to hear the subdued rustle of box sprigs, and the click of secateurs.'

In 1950 Laurence married Jill's younger sister, Theresa, and had two further children, Daniel and Frances. Living in Lyme Regis, Dorset, they celebrated many of the annual festivals explored in this book, setting off rockets at the stroke of midnight on New Year's Eve, lighting blue and white candles for Candlemas on February 2nd, and decorating eggs at Easter. As readers will discover, the oldest tradition of egg decorating involves first dyeing an egg and then scratching a design into the surface; this was, naturally, the method used to beautiful effect by Whistler.

The adoption of these customs by a mid-20th century family was a self-conscious act. A number of the festivals described within these pages had fallen into disuse before World War Two, and in the Introduction to the book Whistler argued that their revival was desirable – even necessary.

THE ENGLISH FESTIVALS

Easter and Whitsun, in particular, he loathed to see reduced to 'mere feverish Bank Holidays'. Why? Because 'they too have added richness to living, and with the other festivals, greater or lesser, each with a peculiar quality, unique and yet related to those preceding and succeeding, have built up the dance of the year.'

This last phrase is a poet's, and it has the same resonance today as it did seventy years ago. Life is more pressured now than ever before, the grip of materialism stronger. We think of the year in terms of retail cycles or the school calendar. Yet there are plenty of people who are actively looking for a more meaningful approach to the annual round, fostering the revival of traditions both local and national. Take, for instance, the wassailing of the apple trees, a Twelfth Night custom mentioned only briefly in these pages and, indeed, almost extinct in the mid-20th century, but today celebrated with gusto not only in its traditional West Country heartland but all over the country.

He might never have imagined this, but Laurence Whistler certainly did believe that annual festivals both ancient (Rogationtide) and more recent (Guy Fawkes Day) could and should be encouraged. What makes this book so enduringly important is that it is not just a history of the English Festivals, but also a visionary evocation of a deeply ingrained and overwhelmingly joyful culture, and a hands-on guide for anyone who wishes to join in, and celebrate 'the dance of the year'.

James Russell is an independent author, curator and lecturer, specialising in 20th century British art and design. He is also an authority on the history and traditions of orchards and cidermaking.

ACKNOWLEDGEMENTS

The author wishes to thank the many friends who have helped in the making of this book. He is grateful to those who have kindly supplied him with much useful information; to Mr. Ronald Fuller; to Dr. John Johnson, concerning the history of the Valentine and the Christmas Card; to Mr. A. St. H. Brock, in connection with fireworks, and for arranging a private display; to Fr. David Peck, Fr. Patrick McLaughlin, the Rev. D. L. Couper and the Rev. C. V. Taylor, in connection with the four Agricultural Festivals; and to Dr. Vaughan Williams, Miss Sybil Eaton, Mr. Mervyn Bruxner, Mr. Charles Wrinch, Mrs. Alfred Lampson and Mr. Robert Loveday, for their thoughts on the subject of carols.

He is grateful to Mr. C. S. Lewis, Mr. de la Mare, Mr. Rolf Gardiner and Mr. Dylan Thomas for permission to quote from their works; to the G.P.O., and its Librarian, Mr. Drury, for permission to reprint Rex Whistler's Valentine Telegram, and for information; also to Miss Edith Olivier, Miss Butroy and the Hulton Press, Miss Christina Hole, Bishop Furse, Mrs. Alice Wallbank, Mr. T. Bruce Dilks, the Rev. K. E. Cartwright, the Chester County Librarian, and the Newcastle-on-Tyne City Librarian; and to the Rev. Andrew Young and Mr. Christopher Hassall. Lastly, he is particularly grateful to Sir Edward Marsh and Canon Hugh Elliott for reading the book in manuscript.

Acknowledgement is made to the Editors of *Country Life*, *The Spectator*, the *English Life Publications*, and *The Windmill*, in whose periodicals some parts of this work have already appeared.

L. W.

CONTENTS

A*

CONTENTS

ILLUSTRATIONS

The head- and tail-pieces are by
Robin Jaques.

INTRODUCTION

*He gives them the seasons, each season different yet every year
the same, so that spring is always felt as a novelty yet always as
the recurrence of an immemorial theme. He gives them in His
Church a spiritual year; they change from a fast to a feast, but
it is the same feast as before.*

C. S. LEWIS—*The Screwtape Letters*

I

THE festivals of the English people acknowledge their
ancestry. One is more pagan in character, another more
Christian, but there are few, if we inspect them closely
enough, which are not seen to be both. There is hardly a
popular feast or fast of the Church that is not remembered in
customs older than the Church—even the crosses on the
buns of Good Friday precede the Cross, in earthly time.
There is hardly a carnival of the primitive world that has not
been tinged with Christian meaning—even on May Day a
hymn is sung on a tower at sunrise. This interpenetration of
old and new is not confined to the customs of England: it
occurred wherever the Gospel was taken, and the Church
finally accepted the necessity of it, approved or at least
condoned it. No doubt it had occurred in Roman Britain,
but the evidence amounts to little. For the festivals of
modern England the outstandingly important year was 597,
when St. Augustine disembarked with his forty monks on a
mission to the people of Kent.

The Anglo-Saxon invasion had not been the final stage of a
continuous nomadic drift from western Asia. Our

[1]

ancestors had lived on the Baltic coast and in the islands for many hundred years before Christ, possibly for many thousand.* They were farmers before they were pirates, and when they left off raiding, and began to occupy the Roman province, they continued to farm. Like all agricultural races, they derived a great part of their sacred rites from a still more ancient fertility cult—hence the nature of the customs we are keeping at the present time. The Christmas holly and the Easter eggs were "English" before any England existed. But the name requires the inverted commas. Saxon and Norman and Dane are we, as Tennyson said; and to Celt he might have added Iberian, French Huguenot, and Dutch Protestant; for the Englishman's blood is thoroughly mixed. But though children were born to Saxon warrior and British captive, the culture of Roman Britain disappeared, East of the Severn. The British Church, driven back into the mountains of Wales, regarded the intruders with terror and contempt, and declined to make any attempt to convert them. Of the British people who were not killed or ejected, Gildas the chronicler wrote the gloomy valediction: "Some, constrained by famine, come in and surrender themselves to be slaves for ever to the enemy." It is interesting to speculate what happened to them then. They lost their Christianity, it seems; yet they appear to have left the mark of their own earlier paganism on the customs kept, even to this day, in a number of places. No doubt their inherited observances had much in common with those of the invaders. The Cornish Furry Dance and the Saxon Maypole are not very difficult to reconcile. But on the whole it is doubtful if the conquerors' habits were much affected by the conquered. The *heathen* element in our festivals would appear to be largely Nordic. The

* H. M. Chadwick, *The Origin of the English Nation*, 1907.

other element we owe to the second conquest by Rome: not the Rome of the legions then, but the Rome of the priest.

England was converted, from North as well as South, with remarkably little opposition. Not one martyrdom is recorded; and even kings who declined baptism refrained from persecuting. The temple priests appear to have been lacking in power and faith. Coifi, the high priest of Odin, according to the famous story in Bede, grumbled that neither the gods nor the king had rewarded him for his pains, and therewith led the attack on his own temple. To explain this remarkable tolerance, in a people ruthless enough on the battlefield, we must bear in mind that the embryo-English were colonials. Their gods were the gods of the old country, immemorially established in particular places, particular shrines. In addition, the Nordics were never a priest-ridden race like the Celts—Julius Cæsar had remarked on the difference. Their gods had been comparatively easy to serve even on the mainland: brought to an island peopled with ghosts of the defeated, haunted at grove and spring by spirits more ardent than themselves, they lacked conviction. And now, confronted with the Good News of the Gospel, they had nothing to say. "If," observed a councillor to the King of Northumbria, "this new learning can inform us of any better surety, methinks it is worthy to be followed."*

But it is one thing to replace the beliefs of a primitive people, and quite another to deprive them of their customs. The Church was already aware of that before she set out to recapture the lost province. Among the letters of encouragement sent by the Pope to St. Augustine, by way of dictating

* The Venerable Bede, *History of the Churche of Englande:* Thomas Stapleton's translation, 1565.

[3]

or suggesting a policy, there occurs the following passage: "When God shall bring you unto our reverend brother Augustine, bishop, tell him what I have long time devised with myself of the cause of the English men. That is to wit that not the temples of the Idols, but the Idols which be in them be broken . For if the said churches be well made, it is needful that they be altered from the worshipping of devils into the service of God; that whilst the people doth not see their temples spoiled, they may (forsaking their error) be moved the more oft to haunt their wonted place to the honour and service of God. And for that they are wont to kill oxen in sacrifice to the devils, they shall use the same slaughter now, but changed to a better purpose. It may therefore be permitted them, that in the dedication days or other solemn days of martyrs, they make to them bowers about their churches, and feasting together after a good religious sort, kill their oxen now to the refreshing of themselves, to the praise of God, and increase of charity, which before they were wont to offer up in sacrifice to the devils: that whilst some outward comforts are reserved unto them, they may thereby be brought the rather to the inward comforts of grace in God. For it is doubtless impossible from men being so rooted in evil customs to cut off all their abuses upon the sudden."*

A wise policy, but with an outcome that the great St. Gregory may not clearly have foreseen; though did he foresee it he may well have concluded that no other advice could be given. In the event, it proved possible to cut off very little. The Anglo-Saxons were gradually cured of their most boorish habits, but the greater part of their customs were never discarded, they were simply endowed with a new significance. At Christmas, Easter and Whitsun, on the

* Bede, Bk. i, Ch. 30.

[4]

anniversary of a patron saint, and on a score of other sacred occasions, the people continued to rehearse their primitive rites, as in part they rehearse them to this day. And interspersed with the events of the Christian calendar there were others on which the impact of the faith was extremely light—May Day and the Harvest, the rituals of the Summer Solstice and the Autumn Equinox; these the Church never seriously attempted to dispute. Thus, at the close of the Middle Ages, there existed an immense agglomeration of sacred and secular customs, in origin almost wholly idolatrous, but from an ecclesiastical point of view, in theory if not in practice, largely redeemed.

The customs of the people had never been denounced so roundly as they were by the Puritans in Stuart England, but that is not to say that they had never been denounced. In the thirteenth century, for example, the Bishop of Salisbury had tried to prevent his flock from abusing those "bowers about their churches", authorised by the Pope six centuries before. Using words that seem to belong to a later period, he forbad all "dances and vile and indecorous games which tempt to unseemliness". Yet the old moralist differed from the new, none the less. Venturing on a generalisation, we may say that reformers who stood, or believed that they stood, within the Catholic tradition, both before and after the Reformation, were anxious to correct the abuse of merriment; whereas the English followers of Calvin were opposed to merriment itself.

' Merry England ' is thought to exist in romantic legend rather than in history; yet the epithet was often used in the fifteenth and sixteenth centuries, and it is clear that the Tudor Englishman believed himself to be rather conspicuously merry, an opinion shared by foreigners. But the word may have been tarnished in the passage of time. Miss

Jameson suggests that the true equivalent would be 'high-hearted',* and it would seem that the translators of the Bible had some such definition or connotation in mind when they declared: "All the days of the afflicted are evil: but he that is of a merry heart hath a continual feast." Since a man can have a mistakenly rosy idea of his fellow-countrymen, it is more illuminating to see the contemporary Englishman imaged in the minds of foreign visitors. They loved us no better than they love us now; therefore anything agreeable they may have had to say is more likely to be just. Of all our visitors in the sixteenth century few can have disliked us more than the young Frenchman, Maistre Perlin, who has little that is pleasant to report except that "Les Angloys, les uns avec les autres, sont joyeux et ayment fort la musique".† He was speaking, as it happened, of Church music; but our reputation abroad was much greater in other branches of the art, and indeed unrivalled. Foreigners wrote well or ill of us according to temperament and experience, but an interesting fact emerges from a study of their opinions: not one of them seems to have found us in any way remarkable for reticence; on the contrary they were nearly all impressed by our love of display in one form or another. Where else but in England, for example, was a stranger not merely allowed but expected, not merely expected but invited, to greet his hostess and her daughters with a kiss on the lips? In a delightful letter, as flattering as we could wish, Erasmus had told a friend of this pleasing custom "it would be impossible to praise too much"—and one which was not outgrown, by the way, until the time of the Commonwealth.—"Wherever you go everyone welcomes you with a kiss, and the same on bidding farewell.

* Storm Jameson, *The Decline of Merry England*, p. 11.

† E. Perlin, *Description d'Angleterre et d'Escosse*, Paris, 1558.

INTRODUCTION

You call again, when there is more kissing   you meet
an acquaintance anywhere and you are kissed till you are
tired. In short, turn where you will, there are kisses,
kisses everywhere. And if you were once to taste them, and
find how delicate and fragrant they are, you would certainly
desire, not for ten years only, like Solon, but to death, to be
a sojourner in England."* Sixty years later Lemmius, a
Dutch doctor, wrote of "the incredible courtesie and
frendlines of speache and affability used in this famous
realme"; but he, like Erasmus, had moved among the
educated, and the humble foreigner was not always so
warmly received. For a balanced opinion we could not
improve on the words of Paul Hentzner, a German visitor
of 1598. "The English," he says, "are grave, like the Germans,
lovers of show.   . . They excel in dancing and music; for
they are active and lively, though of a thicker make than
the French.   They are powerful in the field, successful
against their enemies, impatient of anything like slavery;
vastly fond of great noises that fill the ear, such as the firing
of cannon, drums, and the ringing of bells; so that in
London it is common for a number of them that have got a
glass in their heads to go up into some belfry, and ring the
bells for hours together, for the sake of exercise. If they
see a foreigner very well made, or particularly handsome,
they will say: 'It is a pity he is not an Englishman'." Taking
all opinions into account, we conclude that our ancestors
resembled ourselves in being good-natured, insular and
solid, but differed from us in their ability to be merry
without reserve. Perhaps only the modern Londoner
retains this quality in any marked degree—paradoxically, for
London was shortly to become a centre of Puritanism.

* This quotation and those that follow are derived from W. B. Rye, *England
as Seen by Foreigners in the Days of Elizabeth and James I*, 1865.

[7]

It is worth noticing how widely the old and the new ideas diverged on the subject of children. "A Child," in the charming "Character" written by John Earle, afterwards Bishop of Salisbury,* "Is a Man in a small Letter, yet the best copy of Adam before he tasted of Eve or the apple, and he is happy whose small practice in the world can only write this Character. . He is purely happy, because he knows no evil, nor hath made means by sin to be acquainted with misery. . He is the Christian's example, and the old man's relapse; the one imitates his pureness, and the other falls into his simplicity. Could he put off his body with his little coat, he had got eternity without a burthen, and exchanged but one Heaven for another". It may be that Earle, tender-hearted and tolerant man that he was, underestimated both the miseries of childhood and the force of Original Sin, yet if these words are by no means Catholic doctrine, they are written by one who stood within the old tradition. The Puritan view had been expressed by the master himself. "Even infants," Calvin had pronounced, "though they have not yet brought forth the fruits of their iniquity, they have its seed within them; nay, their whole nature is as it were a seed-bed of sin, and therefore cannot but be odious and abominable to God."†

Clearly this attitude must result in strong ideas on the best upbringing for children, a question related to the subject of this book. James Janeway, the Nonconformist divine, was one who applied them.‡ "Come, tell me truly," he demands of the open-eyed infant, "for I would fain do what I can to keep thee from falling into *everlasting* Fire—How dost thou spend thy time? Is it in Play and Idleness with wicked children? Do you dare to run up and down upon the

---

* John Earle, *Microcosmographie*, 1628.
† Jean Calvin, *Institutes of the Christian Religion*, Bk. 2, Ch. 1, Sec. VIII.
‡ James Janeway, *A Token for Children*, 1671.

Lord's Day? Or do you keep in to read your Book?" He was himself the author of a little book, simply written, specially well suited to a Sabbath evening. It was a story-book, and these were a few of the stories it told: "Of a notorious wicked Child that was taken up from Begging and admirably converted"—"Of a little girl that was Wrought Upon when she was between four and five years old"—"Of a Child that was Very Serious at four years old; with an Account of his comfortable Death when he was twelve."

There was of course a danger in this kind of technique, and a word had been found for it: backsliding. A child might be wrought upon for fifteen years with every sign of success, and then would come a day—a fine Whitsun or Easter—when drum and pipe and jigging fiddle passed under the window. The eyes would be lifted up out of Lamentations, the book would be laid aside, and its owner would take himself off to the marketplace to mingle uneasily with the sons of Mr. Blind-man and Mr. Hold-the-world. On days of this kind the fusion of joy and guilt was accomplished so well that now, if we could rummage in the souls of thousands of our fellow countrymen, we should find there no joy at all that is not uneasy.

But in the present century, when no one defends the Puritan, he cannot be very good sport for long. In the end we must treat him deferentially, for he deserves respect. He was one for whom the reform of the Church of England had been arrested too soon, for whom her doctrines and ceremonies were imbued with idolatry, and the behaviour of the people on feast days and other holidays a public scandal. He was one, we may hazard, for whom the advice of St. Gregory had been wrong from the start. But so far we have only considered his objection to merriment on religious grounds. He had another. Puritanism was the faith of the middle class fighting for power against privilege. "Freeholders and Tradesmen are the strength of religion in this land," declared Richard Baxter,* and thrift and industry were their special virtues. "Among the Reformed, the greater their zeal, the greater their inclination to trade, as holding idleness unlawful."† Thrift and industry in the old England had been considerably less in evidence. Between work and play a balance had been struck that would astonish the modern labourer. In the twentieth century a fortnight in August and the six Bank Holidays are all that the average Englishman is trained to expect. But in the twelfth, according to Walter de Henry, the holidays of the peasant amounted to eight weeks in the year. Certainly, the mediæval conception of a holiday is not our own. In truth it was a holy day, a feast of the Church, though from the moment when the doors were opened after Mass there was nothing of holiness in the way it was kept. If it were one of the great festivals there would be little or no work till the octave was out. If it were the greatest of all there would be none for the "twelve days", and often not very much for forty, till the decorations came down at Candlemas. But the Englishman stayed at home, and contrived his own entertainment from the Church Ale and the village green—or he left the squalor of the village to seek, in the local township, urban pleasures only a degree more urbane. He had no wish for a 'change of scene' nor the means to accomplish it, and he desired nothing less than to spend his leisure by the rude and meaningless sea.

Thus the Puritan onslaught on the festivals was doubly inspired. "Why," demanded Philip Stubbes, the Elizabethan trouncer of abuses, himself no Puritan in the full and

* *Reliquiæ Baxterianæ*, 1696.
† *The Present Interest of England*, 1671, quoted by R. H. Tawney, *Religion and the Rise of Capitalism*, 1929, p. 206.

subsequent sense of the word, "why should they abstaine from bodely labour, peradventure the whole week, spending it in——" and here he enumerated the vices that were undoubtedly countenanced on that holiday.* A nineteenth century manufacturer might have echoed his words (had the poor not been deprived of nearly all their holidays in the interval). "Why should they abstain from labour a whole week?"—but there he would probably have stopped, for the creed of efficiency would have inspired no moral observations, except in so far as a drunken man is hardly efficient. Both Stubbes and the more extreme Calvinists who followed him would certainly have condemned the degeneration of righteous industry into mechanical efficiency. It is a point in favour of the Puritans that they were, after all, more deeply concerned with depravity than with idleness.

Leisure was already diminishing before the extremists achieved any power. Though not opposed to the keeping of festivals in moderation, and though still insisting that her red letter days and black letter days should be holidays— they continued to be so until the time of the Civil War— the Church of England had weeded her calendar vigorously, and expelled a large number of saints. The gain to industry and the corresponding loss to idleness were no doubt, in the long run, of advantage to an island that had to compete in the sharpening economy of Europe, but in the opinion of the Jacobean Puritans the process had been halted altogether too soon. Many of the magistrates were by then of the new persuasion. They could not, of course, compel the Englishman to stay at home on Sunday, or to stay at work on the ancient holidays, but they had the power to curtail his enjoyment. Churchyard amusements on Sunday

* Philip Stubbes, *Anatomie of Abuses*, 1583, p. 153.

evening were suppressed, and when the wandering musicians entered a town at festival time, they were likely to be arrested and fined. Complaints were made to the King during his Progress through Lancashire in 1618, and he determined to take action in defence of "lawful recreations and decent exercises". No doubt he was moved to this by the survival in the North of a large number of Roman Catholics, a perpetual source of disquiet to the Government. Clearly there could be little hope of converting the peasantry if it appeared that merriment went out with the old religion. King James's *Book of Sports* appeared in the form of a Declaration, to be read from every pulpit. "With Our owne Eares Wee have heard the generall complaint of Our people, that they were barred from all lawfull Recreation and exercise upon the Sundayes afternoone, after the ending of all Divine Service, which cannot but produce two evils . perswading them that no honest mirth or recreation is lawfull or tollerable in Our Religion, which cannot but breed a great discontentment in Our peoples hearts. . . The other inconvenience is, that this prohibition barreth the common and meaner sort of people from using such exercises as may make their bodies more able for Warre, when We or Our Successors shall have occasion to use them. And in place thereof sets up filthy tipplings and drunkennesse and breeds a number of idle and discontented speaches in their Alehouses. For when shal the common people have leave to exercise, if not upon the Sundayes and Holydayes, seeing they must apply their labour and winne their living in all working days?"

The following amusements were sanctioned by the *Book of Sports*: dancing, archery, leaping and vaulting, May games, Maypoles, Whitsun Ales and Morris Dancing, and the decorating of churches. The book was reissued in 1633, and once again all clergymen were instructed to read its articles aloud to their congregations. Whether they all did so is open to question, for by this time there were many who were determined to suppress these vanities, and they were strongly supported in Parliament. Their opportunity came in the following decade; for in 1644 Parliament prohibited the keeping of Christmas. Three years later it removed "all festivals or Holy-Dayes, heretofore superstitiously used and observed". March 10th was appointed a day of "public humiliation for the nation's errors of popery, superstition, heresy, schism, and profaneness", and by way of concession every second Tuesday of the month was set apart for recreation. There followed shortly the suppression of the Theatre, in conformity with Stubbes' opinion that plays of every kind, whether sacred or secular, were "quite contrarie to the Word of Grace and sucked out of the Devills teates".— Music, too, for was not "the bringing in of musick a cup of poyson to all the world"? Then in 1651 an Act was passed for the pulling down of all cathedrals, the great homes of music and ceremony, and a beginning was made at Lichfield; but mercifully that folly was not pursued. Inevitably the people resisted; for habits cannot be abolished by Act of Parliament. Holly and rosemary continued to appear on the pulpits of London, and when the officers of the law arrived to ungarnish them they were chased from the streets. There were riots on Christmas Day. And there was much lamentation for the 'good old times', uttered in anonymous pamphlets. "Any man or woman," pleads the author of *An Hue and Cry after Christmas*, "that can give any knowledge of an old, old, very old gray-bearded gentleman, called Christmas, who was wont to be a verie familiar ghest, and visite all sorts of people, both pore and rich, and used to appear in glittering gold, silk, and silver, in the Court, and in all shapes in the Theatre in Whitehall; whosoever can tel what is become of him, or where he may be found, let them bring him back againe into England."*

He was found, of course, not merely in the Court of Charles II, returning out of exile, but in the hearts of most Englishmen, including many of those who had fought for the Parliament. With Charles it seemed that the old England had returned. The festivals were ostentatiously kept, the Maypoles replanted—a very large one in the Strand—and the theatres reopened, or new theatres were built. But too many changes had been wrought in English life for the return to be more than superficial. English music, for example, had suffered a blow from which it has never recovered. We may in this century have become once more a people who *enjoy* good music, but that, alas, is not to say that we are a people who can make it, with our fingers or vocal chords. There would be no revival of dancing after Evensong: the 'English Sunday' had come to stay. Many holidays had been lost outright. Christmas remained, but the 'twelve days' had vanished, or they lingered in the more backward parts of the country, to be finally reduced by the pressure of industry. In 1717 a shrewd politician observed: "The superstition of their religion obligeth France to keep (at least) fifty Holy Days more than we are obliged to keep; and every such day wherein no work is done is one hundred and twenty thousand pounds loss to this deluded people"†—a fair example of the fatuous employment of statistics, for it left out of account both the spiritual and social value of those days, considerations that might be worthy to rank

* *The Arraignment, Conviction and Imprisoning of Christmas   with an Hue and Cry after Christmas*, London, 1646.

† Lawrence Braddon, *Abstract of the draft of a Bill for relieving, reforming and employing the poor*, 1717, quoted R. H. Tawney, *Religion and the Rise of Capitalism*, p. 318.

with finance, though of a kind that we rather ponderously call imponderable.

The seventeenth century had unique importance in the history of our festivals. Never before nor since have they been officially denounced and defended, deliberately abolished and restored. They survived, and they did not survive; the issue was not closed. Their subsequent decline can be attributed in some part to the same opposition, continued under a different name. For in the eighteenth century, while the Church of England, in its Catholic aspect the true guardian of gaiety, was sleeping, Dissent was sharply awake, and the Dissenters inherited much from the Puritan movement: the dread of idolatry, the suspicion of pleasure, the contempt for idleness, and the exaltation of hard work and plain living: a strength and a weakness afterwards shared by the Evangelical party in the Church. But the influence of religion was small in comparison with that of the greatest upheaval in modern history, the revolution in agriculture and industry. For the dispossessed freeholders in the country, the new class of landless workers, and for the immense uprooted proletariate in the towns, labour was becoming, not inevitably more soul-destroying, though sometimes that as well, but more and more an economic and less and less a spiritual activity. Mutual respect between master and man was decaying as they drifted apart: the kitchen was becoming too dainty for the ploughman's boots; the factory owner lived in another world. Without idealising the lot of the former labouring man, which had been at all times oppressively hard, we may say that he had felt himself to be more of a collaborator and less of an employee; and it was collaboration in work and play that nourished the festivals. Now, too, organised sport was taking the place of home-made pleasures, and later a holiday would mean a shutting up of the home, and the derivation of the word would be forgotten.

II

English children, when they are asked to name the most important day in the year, generally answer Christmas, though some may regard a birthday as very little inferior. These are now the main festivals of childhood. Their pleasures may not differ in degree from those of a picnic, a day on the sands or a visit to the theatre, undated and occasional holidays, but they differ in kind, for they are the pleasures of ceremony. Small children are fond of repetition; if a new game catches their fancy, nothing contents them but to have it repeated. Like all of us they want to possess joy absolutely: they wish for eternity and are baffled by time. They are not yet reconciled to the discomfort of impermanence, and they set up their little sequences of reiteration to assuage it. They find in a repeated pleasure the nearest approach to an eternal; and not only will they listen to a gramophone record many times in succession, but at the same hour on the following day they will ask for it again. Their life is continually forming itself into rituals, and they are more at home in orderly than in chaotic surroundings. There is the ritual of waking and dressing, the ritual of nursery and school, of afternoon walk and of evening games, and most compulsive of all, there is the ritual of bedtime, when the day—that epitome of life— being finished, and animal energy used up, the sense of impermanence becomes acute.

Children are content with what they know and like until a new and apparently better idea is suggested. Mercifully for the soon-wearying adult, a show of enthusiasm is enough to convince them that it will indeed be better. For a moment they resist, then they adopt the novelty, and if it appeals to them a great deal they will wish that it may recur. Rigid adherence to ritual is no doubt one sign of insecurity in children, and that again of a failure in love and harmony at home, but the wise parent indulges a normal liking for ritual, and at the same time varies it, instinctively aware, and perhaps without ever considering the matter, that the joys of pure novelty and the joys of pure repetition are both subject to the law of diminishing returns. But since the mere process of adding Summer to Winter, and inch to inch, involves unending alteration of habits, the danger of too much repetition is small, and if there is any conscious thought on the question it needs to be directed against the danger of too much novelty.

The relevance of the epigraph chosen for this Introduction is more apparent when the words are read in their context. For the benefit of readers who are unfamiliar with *The Screwtape Letters*, we must explain that they are supposed to have been written by a senior devil in Hell to a junior and none too competent tempter on earth. The Enemy referred to is God.

"The humans live in time, and experience reality successively. To experience much of it, therefore, they must experience many different things; in other words, they must experience change. And since they need change, the Enemy (being a hedonist at heart) has made change pleasurable to them, just as He has made eating pleasurable. But since He does not want them to make change, any more than eating, an end in itself, He has balanced the love of change in them by a love of permanence. He has contrived to gratify both tastes together in the very world He has made, by that union of change and permanence which we call Rhythm. He gives them the seasons, each season different yet every year the same, so that spring is always felt as a novelty, yet always as the recurrence of an immemorial theme. He gives them in His Church a spiritual year; they change from a fast to a feast, but it is the same feast as before.

"Now just as we pick out and exaggerate the pleasure of eating to produce gluttony, so we pick out this natural pleasantness of change and twist it into a demand for absolute novelty. This demand is entirely our workmanship. If we neglect our duty, men will be not only contented but transported by the mixed novelty and familiarity of snow-drops *this* January, sunrise *this* morning, plum pudding *this* Christmas. Children, until we have taught them better, will be perfectly happy with a seasonal round of games in which conkers succeed hopscotch as regularly as autumn follows summer. Only by our incessant efforts is the demand for infinite, or unrhythmical, change kept up."*

Even those who doubt the reality of these Agents for and against us may admit the truth of what is said about human nature; our need in childhood, and indeed throughout life, of "that union of change and permanence which we call Rhythm", which events like Christmas and a birthday so well provide. But Screwtape's observations do not exhaust the meaning of the festivals, nor their value for children. We can have too high an opinion of a child's faculties, though as a rule they are less dulled than those of the mature. A great deal depends on environment and example. A child, an urban child at any rate, can live through the year without any great interest in the change of the seasons, just as a child can experience very little of beauty and creation, of wonder and generosity and gratitude, if his world is poor in these

* C. S. Lewis, *The Screwtape Letters*, XXV.

goods. Christmas invites them. It is one day, and that the chief, which compels awareness of seasonal change, giving to the headlong surge of time the movement of a dance. November ascends to it promisingly. January subsides from it fulfilled. The making and searching for presents, the putting up of holly and ivy on picture and shelf, the enjoyment of the glittering tree—what other event in the year is so evocative of beauty and creation and wonder, of generosity and gratitude? And these encomiums say nothing of the true meaning of Christmas, which even for small children infuses into the scarlet of the berries and the stillness of the flames a quality that has no substitute.

A Winter without Christmas would indeed be poor, and the apprentices of London saw that it would never do. Let us pity the Lowland Scotch, not because they are still Presbyterians, but because they have nothing but a raw-boned Hogmanay to offset the removal of their greatest festival. But there are other festivals, including two great ones, which the English themselves are in danger of losing. In the pagan world the rites of Spring were at least as elaborate as those of the Winter Solstice, origin of Christmas customs, and to the Christian the Resurrection and the gift of the Holy Spirit mean as much as the Nativity. In other words, Easter and Whitsun were once nearly as well kept as Christmas. They were not *quite* as well kept, because the Nativity is easier to imagine, closer to everyday experience and so, in a sense, more 'human'.

Our gain in keeping up Christmas is roughly the measure of our loss if we allow Easter and Whitsun from the social point of view to degenerate into mere feverish Bank Holidays. This fate may be still reserved for Easter; it has almost overtaken Whitsun already. Yet they too have added richness to living, and with the other festivals, greater or lesser, each with a peculiar quality, unique and yet related to those preceding and succeeding, have built up the dance of the year.

Many will admit the value of the festivals, but not that we can do anything to arrest their decline by an effort of will. Old customs deliberately revived, they claim, are anachronisms, and new ones deliberately introduced would be quite without meaning, and in fact the impulse has gone. Indeed, we must recognise the change in manners that has occurred during the last century and a half. The adult English of all classes are more sophisticated than they were and more self-conscious. Perhaps they enjoy life as much as their ancestors, but they are reluctant to show it. Their reserve seldom breaks down. When it does—on a national victory, a Coronation in London, a Guy Fawkes night in Sussex—we all remark on it. They will then dance in the streets, but in a random fashion and without ceremonial. They have lost the power to be spontaneously and formally gay in public. Rubbing shoulders in a crowded island has encouraged a love of privacy, and the festivals they keep have gone indoors. For all the gusto of the English Folk Dance Society, the Morris and the Sword Dance are not likely to catch on. They are 'quaint', and the epithet is lethal. However, this argument does not apply to children.

But to return to the main question, it is untrue that deliberate revival or deliberate introduction of customs can never succeed. As it happens, the general deterioration of the festivals in modern England has coincided with some notable improvements, deliberately brought about. The Christmas tree is not indigenous here, and was quite unknown in England till the nineteenth century. It was introduced by some German families to Manchester, and afterwards, more noticeably, by the Prince Consort at

Windsor Castle in 1841. Within twenty years it had proliferated through the whole of society from the top downwards. Christmas carols were dying out—"carols begin to be spoken of as not belonging to this century," observed Hone in 1825.* They were deliberately revived in the second half of the century, and some of the loveliest and most popular were only snatched from oblivion at the end of it. The candlelit tree and the carols are now, surely, the best loved ingredients of a festival that is better kept than at any time since the Commonwealth.

It is clear that we could have, if we wished, and without danger of artificiality, a better Easter as well, and a better Whitsun, and in fact a better sequence of festivals altogether —provided we had the time and the energy to improve them. Carols are worth considering in this connexion, for they are not confined to Christmas. There were Easter and Whitsun and May carols in the fifteenth century; some of them were still sung by children in the nineteenth; and many can be found in the popular collections. It is clear too that any wish to improve the festivals is likely to be strongest among Christians. The carols are now enjoyed by agnostics, but they were revived as Christian songs. The Christmas tree is in every home, but it would hardly have found its way there without the initiative of those who thought the pleasures of the day worth trouble because they were sanctified. The most popular of country celebrations, the Harvest Thanksgiving, is without historical precedent, a deliberate invention of the Victorian Church; and quite recently the Church of England has strongly revived the three other agricultural festivals, Plough Sunday, Rogationtide and Lammas.

From all these considerations we may conclude that the festivals are not beyond improvement by those who think

* William Hone, *The Every-Day Book*, Vol. I, col. 1599.

B

they are worth improving. They will be persons—to find their common denominator—who have what is called a 'spiritual view' of life: materialism can have nothing to *add* to the festivals, though it may regard them with tolerance. Going further, we may conclude that we could not *invent* traditions in a void: they would fail to become traditional. We should need to take note of what is or has been. The Christmas tree and the Harvest Thanksgiving are no exceptions to this rule, for there had always been Christmas and the evergreens of Christmas, and obviously there had always been thanksgiving services. Finally, we may think that although the reserved Englishman has no gift for spontaneous and public ceremony, his children have, and some occasions —the Harvest itself, for example—may be worth improving for their sakes. But the presence of children is the best excuse for the keeping of any festival.

This book is intended to be a guide to the festivals of England, as they are and might be. It differs from other books on the subject which are wholly concerned with what they were. Since History provides both a source and an explanation, a great many pages are devoted to the past, but the accent falls on the present. The festivals are of the kind already discussed: days that recur, days that can be widely or universally celebrated, days that involve a ritual of enjoyment in their keeping. But perhaps they are easier to define in a negative way, for they vary a good deal in character, and even more in value.

A Bank Holiday is not a festival though widely kept, because there is nothing of ritual about it. The Derby is not a festival, though of general interest, for it could only constitute a 'ritual occasion' to those who attend it. For the same reason we exclude the Malvern Festival and the Three Choirs Festival at Gloucester, Worcester or Hereford—

the oldest musical event of its kind in Europe—and should have no concern with the ceremony at Stratford if it were not now the most notable feature and the best reminder of St. George's Day. Then the feasts of the Church and the other days named in her calendar, these too are beyond our concern when they are purely sacred events, like Trinity Sunday, and when, unlike Christmas, Easter and Whitsun, they suggest no secular way of keeping them.* As for the ceremonies of State, the Lord Mayor's Show, the Trooping of the Colour, and the Opening of Parliament, they are spectacles, and the part of the spectator is a passive one.

The 'Year Book' or 'Book of Days', familiar to other generations, provided the model for the present work, but unlike them it begins at Christmas, at the Nativity and the Winter Solstice, the true beginning of the cycle in so far as a continuous rhythm can be said to have any beginning. Twenty-four public events are described, together with three private ones—a Christening, a Wedding and a Birthday. Among the festivals one fast will be found, for any account of the cycle must contain a chapter on Good Friday. Some might be inclined to omit one or two of the minor events that are included, or even perhaps to replace them with others that have been omitted, though that is less probable. The writer can only offer the evidence that each day is alive, well aware that some are of great importance, and others of little. But length of chapter is not a reliable guide to importance. Midsummer, for example, is no longer a notable occasion, and many of those pages are devoted to an account of fireworks. It would have been possible to vary the size of the type in accordance with the size of the festivals; but then, if the Christmas chapters were printed in

* An exception is made in the case of Lammas, for a reason given in that chapter.

Pica, a just sense of proportion would allow Guy Fawkes nothing larger than Nonpareil, and what would remain for St. Michael and all his Host but an ignominious Minikin?

A very long chapter could be written on every one of the days selected, so rich are they in custom and legend, searched out and described again by generations of notable men from the credulous Aubrey to the analytical Frazer. While recording the past, the writer has attempted to emphasise certain traditions that are valuable. Not much will be found on the subject of pure superstitions, Father Christmas excepted; it would be no less futile than misguided to wish to resuscitate them. Nor has any attempt been made to include every variant of custom known to the connoisseur of these things: local customs of the past and present are only described when they appear to be of general interest. How, then, shall we define the valuable tradition? It is one with a green end, or one that conceivably might, if attended to, and for all its moribund appearance, venture a leaf.

THE GROWTH OF
ENGLISH CHRISTMAS

*It was a strange figure—like a child; yet not so like a child as
like an old man, viewed through some supernatural medium.*
CHARLES DICKENS—*A Christmas Carol*

CHRISTMAS DAY stands to the New Year as a wedding in
a church to one in a registry office. At this season begins
the cycle of life, a cycle observed in some fashion by
everyone to whom Christmas and Easter and Whitsun are
days of importance in the year, if only as holidays. Fortunately they are more than that to most of us, and their true
meaning cannot be disregarded in this book, even though it
is principally concerned with certain domestic and social
customs, which the fasts and feasts of the Church have
gathered about them, like a coat of many colours, worn to
make the naked meaning more attractive. It need hardly
be said, one would think, that if coat and meaning are parted,
the meaning may be able to survive, but the coat will not.
It will continue unmended, steadily becoming more
unfashionable, until the time arrives for us to throw it away.
For whether we care to admit it or not, it is the meaning
which keeps it fresh and in the fashion—which inspires us
to patch or replace it from time to time. In plain words,
the unbeliever (though here we must not attempt too
precise a definition of belief) who enjoys keeping Christmas
in style is living on capital. If all were like him, there would
ultimately be no Christmas to keep.

Advent is the time of preparation for Christmas, in the

secular as in the religious sense; the time in which presents are bought and made, good food and drink laid in, carols sung, a Christmas tree prepared, holly and mistletoe looked for, churches and houses decorated. Many of these customs are very old—so old that the entire recorded part of human history has occurred since they came into being, no one knows where or when. At Midwinter, when the hours of daylight were fewest, the warmth of the sun weakest, and life itself seemingly at a standstill, our ancestors, the archaic peoples of Europe and Western Asia, kept festival by lighting bonfires and decorating their buildings with evergreens. They did so, according to the anthropologist, out of a savage belief that the dying sun could be enheartened by imitative fire, and the life of the buried seed assured by the ritual use of branches, evergreen branches that were lively even in the dead season; and these practices and others like them have been called acts of imitative magic. Yet it may be that the childhood of the race acquired, or retained, glimpses of spiritual truth beyond the comprehension of a tidy and complacent rationalism. However we interpret the facts, it is certainly true that the customs of primitive peoples resemble each other so strongly as to indicate a common source, coeval perhaps with human life. In Europe, the ancient civilised world received from that source a rich legacy of ceremonial, and passed it on with little attenuation to Christendom; so that the Spring Gods became identified with Christ, and the birthday of the sun with the birthday of the Light of the World.

He was born into that afternoon age of Rome which had replaced the early magic of the Winter Solstice with the splendid though decaying festival of the Saturnalia, a week of riotous holiday-making when master and servant changed places, presents were given, and evergreen garlands worn.

But the Divine Birthday was honoured under many names, and the Romans collected interpretations of divinity. Saturn's birthday was also the birthday of Attis and Mithras— Mithras the god of the Roman soldier, and for a time (it seemed) a dangerous rival to the new God out of Palestine; while in the North the barbarians were keeping the long festival of Yule. Thus December 25th was everywhere, in effect, *Dies Natalis Invicti Solis*, the Birthday of the Unconquered Sun.

"Let those who have no light in themselves light candles!" said Tertullian.* "Let those over whom Hell fire is hanging fix to their doors laurels doomed presently to burn! You are the light of the world, you are the tree ever green. If you have renounced temples, make not your own house a temple." So did one of the greatest of the early fathers direct—before the conservatism of the heathen recommended a change of policy. St. Gregory's advice to St. Augustine, four centuries later, has already been recorded in the Introduction to this book. Presently the words *"templa exornantur"* began to appear beside Christmas Eve in the calendars of the Church, reversing the judgment of Tertullian. Christmas decorations had received baptism. "Against the feast of Christmas, every man's house, as also their parish churches, were decked with holme, ivie, bayes, and whatsoever the season of the yeare afforded to be greene: The Conduits and Standardes in the streets were likewise garnished."† Neither the puritans of the first three centuries, nor those of the seventeenth, proved strong enough to abolish the evergreens of Yule.

One evergreen alone has never been truly baptised, and is seldom used in churches at the present time. The mistletoe

---

* Tertullian, Treatise *Of Idolatry*, VII, xv.
† John Stow, *Survey of London*, 1598, 'Sports and Pastimes.'

still holds in its unredeemed pale berries a shred of its meaning in a world in which it was the Golden Bough—–the plant which killed Baldur the Beautiful—the plant which a druid cut from the parent oak, it is said, ceremoniously at the Winter Solstice, using a long gold-handled knife or sickle, then handed to the people with the words, "the mistletoe of the New Year". For it is 'All Heal', the magic bough under which enemies were reconciled. When some of these helpful but unholy twigs were brought into a church near London in the eighteenth century, the clergyman at once ordered them to be thrown out. Why then were they allowed in York Cathedral? For Brand tells us "they carry mistletoe to the high altar of the cathedral and proclaim a public and universal liberty, pardon, and freedom to all sorts of inferior and even wicked people at the gates of the city, towards the four quarters of heaven".* The explanation can only be that in York the druidic tradition was very strong. In general belief the mistletoe was a "heathenish and profane plant", and therefore much better suited to the private dwellings of Christians.

The Christmas tree in Germany may be no less ancient than the mistletoe bough in Britain. We might see in it a custom of the Saturnalia introduced by the Roman legions, the pine tree hung with little masks of Bacchus: "*Oscilla ex alta suspendunt mollia pinu.*"† But the decorated tree is more likely to have been a barbarian usage already. Since Luther delighted in Christmas and all its gaieties, many Lutherans believe that he invented the custom. The tree was undoubtedly Lutheran in the early part of the nineteenth century, and though it has been adopted since then by the German Catholics, it has made very little headway among

---

* See William Hone, *The Every-Day Book*, Vol. I, col. 1637.
† Georgics II, 389.

the Latin peoples. In 1798 Coleridge spent Christmas at Ratzeburg in North Germany, and has left us in *The Friend* a charming account of a very Teutonic scene.

"There is a Christmas custom here which pleased and interested me. The children make little presents to their parents, and to each other, and the parents to their children.

On the evening before Christmas-day, one of the parlours is lighted up by the children, into which the parents must not go; a great yew bough is fastened on the table at a little distance from the wall, a multitude of little tapers are fixed in the bough, but not so as to burn it till they are nearly consumed, and coloured paper, etc., hangs and flutters from the twigs. Under this bough the children lay out in great order the presents they mean for their parents, still concealing in their pockets what they intend for each other. Then the parents are introduced, and each presents his little gift; they then bring out the remainder one by one, from their pockets, and present them with kisses and embraces. Where I witnessed this scene, there were eight or nine children, and the eldest daughter and the mother wept aloud for joy and tenderness; and the tears ran down the face of the father, and he clasped all his children so tight to his breast, it seemed as if he did it to stifle the sob that was rising within it. I was very much affected. The shadow of the bough and its appendages on the wall, and arching over on the ceiling, made a pretty picture; and then the raptures of the *very* little ones, when at last the twigs and their needles began to take fire and *snap*—O it was a delight to them!"

Prince Albert's Christmas tree at Windsor in 1841 was not, as many imagine, the first to be seen in this country. One had been lit for a party of English children at least twenty years before, by a German of Queen Caroline's

B*

household;* another, or rather three others, by the Princess Lieven, staying at Panshanger for Christmas in 1829. A fellow-guest in the house was Charles Greville, who fully recorded the scene in his *Memoirs*. "It was very pretty. Here it was only for the children; in Germany the custom extends to persons of all ages." A Swiss governess introduced the tree to a third English household in 1831,† and still another visitor to keep Christmas in the German way was the Baron Bunsen at Llanover in 1838.‡ It would be strange if these were the only examples. It would be stranger still if none of the English families who witnessed it adopted the ceremony themselves in later years. They certainly did at Manchester, where a number of German merchants had settled by this time. William Howitt reported in 1840, "it is spreading fast among the English there—pine tops being brought to market for the purpose, which are generally illuminated with a taper for every day in the year"§—perhaps a numerical exaggeration.

Still, no mention is made of the tree in *The Comic Almanack* of this date, a very full account of contemporary Christmas gaieties by Cruickshank and 'Rigdum Funnidos', or in any other Christmas book, it seems, published before 1841; and we may doubt if it would so soon, or indeed ever, have become the property of everyone, but for the publicity it acquired by appearing at Court—for publicity established it; not affection for Germany. We might suppose that the Queen's happy marriage encouraged the people to think tenderly of German habits. We might suppose that in a period when one half of society could remember the excitement after Waterloo, and when, for the other half,

---

* Loseley MSS, ed. A. J. Kempe, 1836, p. 75.

† Georgiana, Baroness Bloomfield, *Reminiscences*, 1883, Vol. I, p. 6.

‡ *Notes and Queries*, 7th Series, XII, 492.

§ *The Rural Life of England*, 2nd ed., 1840, p. 461.

the delicious terror of 'Boney' was not forgotten—a small and fading ghost conjured by the nurse in the shadows of the nursery curtains—the old ally would be kindly regarded. History will not allow it. The Germans were laughed at, the Prince coolly received. But the young Queen's happiness and growing family were on all sides approved, and the details of family life at Windsor aroused affectionate interest. Two months before Christmas a Prince of Wales had been born: that was why Albert kept high festival, and why the Christmas tree appeared in the Castle. "This is the dear Christmas Eve," he wrote. "To-day I have two children of my own to give presents to, who, they know not why, are full of happy wonder at the German Christmas-tree and its radiant candles."* Though the Prince was too humourless for the aristocracy, to all England the couple exemplified Christian marriage. We may observe that when the Elector of Hanover arrived with his unloved German ways in 1714, there had been no inclination to adopt them.

For a few Winters the tree reproduced itself within the walls of the Castle. Soon there was one for the Queen (the Prince provided the presents), and one for the Prince (the Queen took charge of this), and one for the children (here they combined), and several for other members of the household, and two in the dining-room. There seem to have been six or eight at least, fully decorated and loaded with trinkets, and Mr. Mawditt, the Queen's confectioner, arranged them all, and was no doubt responsible, as well, for some that were lit in private houses. In a charming lithograph of 1848† we are shown the six royal children with their mother and father grouped around their tree, over six feet high, which stands on a table covered with white

---

* Sir Theodore Martin, *Life of the Prince Consort*.
† In the Rischgitz Collection, now the property of the Hulton Press, Limited.

damask. About the roots the larger toys are arranged—soldiers on horseback, dolls, a chariot, and a railway engine of the period, with tall funnel and large driving wheel. The six tiers of branches are crowded with candles and hung with sweetmeats, bells and paper toys; and on the apex floats an angel with spread wings, holding a wreath in each hand. For the twelve nights of Christmas the trees were kept burning and carefully tended, and guests were conducted from room to room to look at them.

A wider public learnt of the novelty in the pictures and articles of *The Illustrated London News*. This year it reported that "the Christmas tree is somewhat more of a German than an English Custom", and in 1850 it was still to Dickens "the new German toy". But four Christmases later there were hundreds for sale in Covent Garden Market, and a prodigious glittering fir tree on view at the Crystal Palace.* Thus the Christmas tree, reversing the normal procedure, was introduced by the rich to the poor and by the Londoner to the countryman. "Within the last twenty years," Chambers observes in 1864, "the custom has been introduced into England with the greatest success, and must be familiar to most of our readers."† At the same time it had conquered the United States, brought there by the German settlers in Pennsylvania. "We shall have an old-fashioned Christmas," wrote President Harrison in 1891. "The Christmas tree is in almost every home."

A notion is current that the Christmas of old England had been little more than an affair of eating and drinking, of the boar's head and the wassail bowl. But to imagine, as some apparently do, that the Victorians 'invented' the Christmas we know would be folly. The singing of carols, the lighting

---

* *I.L.N.*, 23rd December, 1854.

† R. Chambers, *The Book of Days*, 1864.

of candles, the giving of presents and the decorating with evergreens are all traditional, and most of them indeed immemorial; so too is Father Christmas, impersonated in the hall and on the stage a very long while before any English child had heard mention of Santa Claus. We even possessed an evergreen device, of which more will be said, equivalent in purpose and, in the writer's opinion, equal in beauty to the Christmas tree.

Coleridge appears, it is true, to have found the German custom of giving Christmas presents a novelty; but he can only mean that to him, as an Englishman, the ritual employed was novel. That is evident from a letter addressed to William Hone in 1825.* "Pray remember," says the correspondent, a certain T. N. of Cambridge, "that it is a Christmas custom from time immemorial to send and receive presents and congratulations from one friend to another." This is confirmed by Leigh Hunt, writing for *The Indicator*. The children are returning from school, he says, "in a few days you shall see them, new clothes, warm gloves, gathering round their mother at every toy-shop, claiming the promised bat, hoop, top or marbles"—awaiting too "the expected Christmas-box from Grand-papa and Grand-mama. . . At no season of the year are their holidays so replete with pleasures".† Assuredly there were presents; but it seems that English children do owe to Germany their secret preparation, possibly the ritual of the Christmas stocking, and a pleasantly revivified notion of Father Christmas.

He is old as Europe, and has assumed several names in his time. Once he was Woden, the bringer of gifts, lashing his rein-deer through the darkness of northern midwinter; and

* Included in *The Every-Day Book*, Vol. I, Col. 1606.
† Quoted by Hone, Col. 1607.

who knows what names he may have had in deep Asia, before the tribes moved westwards? Then he encountered the Church. It was at a time when she had abandoned exorcism for prestidigitation. She could not abolish him altogether, therefore she transformed him into a saint, into the much-loved Nicholas, Bishop of Myra in the fourth century. It was one of many conjuring tricks she performed at that period. St. Nicholas became the patron saint of children, and his day was December 6th. It is reported that one of his good acts was to revive three schoolboys murdered by an innkeeper who hid their dismembered bodies in a tub of pickles. He was a rich man who loved giving anonymous presents, and another kindness he did was to throw a purse through a window, after dark, to a poverty-stricken old man who was about to prostitute his three daughters. Perhaps it was on account of this that children began to write little notes sometime before December 6th to tell him about the toys they specially wanted; for these notes were either left on the window sill at night or else on a ledge in the chimney, a wide chimney down which it would be quite easy for him to grope and find them. Then on his appointed day the saint himself—Santa Claus—never failed to appear at the window and distribute his presents, and these the children found—in that condition of mingled belief and scepticism, of astonishment and expectation, which only children experience—to be exactly what they had asked for.

But St. Nicholas Day chanced to lie in the magnetic field of a much more potent festival, and after a while it could not prevent part of its ceremony flying away and adhering to Christmas. Then in Bavaria the children still left their notes on the window sill, but they addressed them to *Liebes Christkind*—Krishkinkle as they knew him—and the saint's part in the matter was simply to deliver the letters in heaven. The Child himself brought the presents to earth with him on Christmas morning, and filled all the stockings he found hanging at the foot of beds. In Scandinavia and parts of Germany he was actually impersonated; here by a boy crowned with nine burning candles on a wreath of leaves; there by a girl with a red sash to her white frock, passing from room to room at cockcrow, to bring everyone a hot drink and good wishes. The ritual of the stocking is not mentioned by Brand or Hone; and the compilers of the Oxford Dictionary found no allusion to it earlier than the year 1854, when a book was published entitled *The Christmas Stocking*, by Susan and Anna Warner, which seems to indicate that the custom was derived from Germany.* Yet it is by no means exclusively Nordic. In certain French and Italian convents the nuns would hang stockings on the abbess' door, with notes inside asking for St. Nicholas' protection; and next morning they would be found to be full of sweets and trinkets.

Father Christmas of modern England owes much to Santa Claus of Germany, but not his existence. He had been, so to speak, one aspect of Woden that escaped canonisation (which alone could have saved his dignity), lost his power to alarm, but preserved and cultivated his geniality. Should anyone doubt whether he is truly historical it would be easy to establish the fact. Five centuries ago we had a carol in England which began "Hail Father Christmas, hail to thee!"; Ben Jonson wrote a masque about him for the court of King James;† and he has always been very

---

* From a correspondence in *Notes and Queries* of 1879 it appears that it was well known but not yet general at that date. It may possibly have been an old English custom, preserved in some parts of the country, and afterwards reintroduced to the rest.

† *Christmas His Masque.*

well known to the countryman as a character in the
Mummers' Play.

> "In comes I, Father Christmas,
>   Welcome or welcome not.
> I hope old Father Christmas
>   Will never be forgot."

An unpretentious fellow was Christmas, with nothing at all
of the saintly about him, and little of the superhuman. He
had travelled far and forgotten a great deal, but where men
loved him he was happy. Who can imagine him to-day,
benignly supernatural, condescending to admit that he
might not be *welcome*! We will take our leave of the
unregenerate immortal as he appeared in 1795 in "A
humourous Pageant of Christmas, personified by an old man
hung round with savoury dishes". Then all was changed.
The fringe of a saint's radiance touched him, and he came to
regard his cummerbund of savoury dishes with contempt.

Christmas customs to-day appeal rather less to the senses
and considerably more to the spirit than did those of the
eighteenth century, yet we cannot ascribe this finally to the
impact of Santa Claus and the Christmas tree, nor to the
enthusiasm of Dickens* for the festival, since these were not
the cause of a spiritual revival, but rather the result. To
that revival we owe the present popularity of carols—the
only national songs to hold their ground against the storms of
fragrant hair-oil that ululate towards us from the crooners of
America. It seems strange to us that carols were once in
danger of dying out, yet that was the case. For two centuries
after the Commonwealth they were never heard in church,
nor in the houses of the well-to-do, but fortunately the

---

* Books that have helped to build up Christmas are Washington Irving's
Sketchbook, Dickens' *Christmas Books*, and *The Tailor of Gloucester* by
Beatrix Potter—all of them excellent Christmas reading for children.

illiterate remembered what the educated had forgotten. Henry Bourne, writing his *Antiquities* in 1725, declared that "it is customary among the common People to sing a Christmas Carol", and he condemned the practice because "to sing it, as is generally done, in the midst of Rioting and Chambering and Wantoness, is no Honour, but Disgrace; no Glory, but an Affront to that Holy Season, a Scandal to Religion, and a sin against Christ". Hone's pronouncement was made exactly a hundred years later.* "Carols begin to be spoken of as not belonging to this century. These ditties, which now exclusively enliven the industrious servant-maid, and the humble labourer, gladdened the festivity of royalty in ancient times." He regarded them as 'quaint' material for the antiquarian. "In the rage for collecting almost everything, it is surprising that collectors have almost overlooked carols as a class of popular poetry." William Howitt was even more definite. Carols, he said, "are not calculated to stand the test of these days; the schoolmaster will root them all out."†

As it happened, the first collection had been made in 1822, by Gilbert Davies, and another, by Sandys, followed in 1833. These collectors agreed with Hone and Howitt that the carols were destined to become extinct. However, they lingered on in humble memory, nourished by perennial broadsheets, until in the second half of the century there began the renascence of English music which is one of the best credentials of our culture. Several factors contributed then to the revival of English carols. One was the desire for beauty in English worship, dominated too long by the droning of the Georgian sermon. Another, oddly enough, was the discovery by Neale and Helmore of a rare book of

* *The Every-Day Book*, Vol. I, Cols. 1599, 1603.
† W. Howitt, *The Rural Life of England*, 1838, Part II, p. 212.

very beautiful sixteenth century *Swedish* tunes, many of which they published in 1853 and 1854, with their own words. Ever since the introduction of Italian Opera it had been easier to arouse interest in foreign music than in English, so unconfident, and indeed ignorant, had we become of our own musical ability, in this island dubbed by the Germans, "*Das Land ohne Musik.*" Thus 'Good King Wenceslas', an alien tune, became popular among the educated, while 'The Holly and the Ivy', indigenous and very ancient, faded from unlettered memory, till Cecil Sharp rescued it, along with 'The Seven Joys of Mary' and many other delightful carols, towards the end of the century. *His* work is a third factor, together with that of his colleagues—men who travelled in the country noting down words and airs, some of extreme loveliness, from the few voices that still remembered them.

A carol is never a hymn; and it has never forgotten that its name once signified a dance. "A ring-dance with song" is the original meaning noted by the Oxford Dictionary, and that is the meaning it held for Chaucer as he wrote *The Romaunt of the Rose* in the fourteenth century.

> 'Come, and if it lykè you
> To dauncen dauncith with us now.'
> And I, withoutè tarrying,
> Wente into the karolying.

There had been, of course, Christian hymns many centuries before Chaucer, but these were not carols; and there had been carols as long or longer, lilting words for dancing to, wanton or merely festive, such as "Blow, northerne wynd Send thou me my sweetyng", but these were not Christian. It was mainly the English Franciscans who in the fourteenth century began to redeem the popular songs of the day, remembering their master's injunction to be *ioculatores Dei*; and thus began the first age of the sacred carols we delight in, though most of them were written, as the editors of *The Oxford Book* express it, "between the death of Chaucer in 1400 and the ejection of the Rev. Robert Herrick from his parish by Oliver Cromwell's men in 1647." Englishmen knew them well in the fifteenth century, and some may even have danced to them in the nights of Christmas, the leader giving the verse, the whole household joining in the easy refrain.*

The carol is the popular song of the faith; a song in which some event of the Gospel story is remembered as if it had happened only yesterday, and described as if it were happening to-day. It may be merry or it may be pathetic, but it is always familiar; and it was this familiarity which offended the Augustans. "Had the author *designed* to have rendered his Subject ridiculous, he could not more effectively have made it so." The beauty, of course, resides in this very gift of making the divine seem commonplace, yet no less wonderful for that. With a force few sermons will ever generate it brings the Incarnation *home*. The Christ is an English child, his Mother a lady of great beauty who dandles him on her knee, and sometimes rebukes him, and sings him to sleep with "Lulla, lulla, lullaby, My sweet little Babe, what meanest thou to cry?" With this and the utter purity of an air the carols move us, and are unlikely to fall into a second eclipse while the language lives.

> To-morrow shall be my dancing day:
> I would my true love so did chance
> To see the legend of my play,

* See E. K. Chambers, *English Literature at the Close of the Middle Ages*, 1945, Chap. II.

To call my true love to my dance.
Sing O my love, O my love, my love,
This have I done for my true love.

In a manger laid and wrapped I was,
So very poor, this was my chance,
Between an ox and a silly poor ass,
To call my true love to my dance.

Then down to hell I took my way
For my true love's deliverance;
And rose again on the third day
Up to my true love and the dance.

Then up to heaven I did ascend
Where now I dwell in sure substance,
At the right hand of God, that men
May come into the general dance.

When with the highest motive the Calvinists "made a breach in the bulwarks of the holy pictures"—to borrow a phrase from Dr. Jung—the first age of the carols came to an end; and in the second the simplicity that created them is hard, if not impossible, to recapture. It is difficult not to sympathise with the Tudor yeoman who grumbled, "it was never mery in Ingland sithens the scriptures were so commonly talked upon among such personnes as they weare."

CHRISTMAS EVE

DECEMBER 24TH

We hang up in the Hall, or &c., a Mistletoe-bough. 'Tis obvious to ghesse how 'tis derived downe to us.
JOHN AUBREY—Remaines of Gentilisme and Judaisme

EVERGREENS are a symbol of undying life, and all are equally suitable except yew, which is proper to Easter. There is no need to confine our choice to holly and mistletoe, and that is worth remembering in a year when berries are few. Ivy, cypress, ilex; laurel, rosemary, bay and box; all these have been used throughout English history; and as Stow observed, the Elizabethan Londoner embellished his house and church with *"whatsoever the Season afforded to be Green"*. The symbolism is deep and manifold. Holly is the Crown of Thorns, already implicit in Christmas Day; its berries are Christ's blood. Holly is masculine, ivy feminine. Ivy is also Bacchus' plant and therefore in former times not wholly in favour. In some counties it was used to decorate the outside of the house, a practice unfortunately no longer kept, now that the festival has gone indoors. Holly bought at a shop is better than none at all, but cannot mean as much to children as the holly they have looked for themselves, climbed for and scratched their fingers on, till the squeak and shine and recalcitrance of it became a possession. The trouble taken is the measure of the meaning. And that is true of the other preparations for Christmas in which towns-children are not so handicapped.

It is an old custom to decorate a part of the parish church, such as the font or the lectern, or the windows of one aisle; and now hot-house flowers are used, in addition to ever-greens. Every feature is treated independently, yet the effect might be better if all would agree to subordinate their ideas to a general design. When the architecture is good the decoration ought to enunciate its lines instead of confusing them, and it would be a mistake to think symmetry dull. All the pillars on the left might be wound with thick spirals of ivy in one direction, and all those on the right in the other. Equal swags of holly might fall each side of the chancel arch or be looped above it, and circular wreaths be placed in the spandrels of the arches. From the crown of the arches spherical lanterns of evergreen could hang, enclosing the electric lights. They are made of four circles of wire intersecting and tied at the 'poles'; the eight 'meridians' thus formed being kept in place by a horizontal 'equator'; and the whole framework is then covered with evergreen. These lanterns look well round any hanging light, whether in church or in the house; but if in the nave the lamp does not hang from the crown of the arch, one large red paper bell might be used. The use of paper in church would not be as original as it sounds. In years gone by, when a boy or girl had died in the parish, a 'Maiden's Garland' was hung up, a crown of white paper with paper roses and streamers, white and blue.

Early Victorian prints reveal that houses were decorated very much as they are to-day, except that evergreens were often more lavishly used, and a room transformed into a bower. Dickens writes of a room "so hung with living green, that it looked a perfect grove". A swag can be made on a centre of straw, the evergreens being bound to it with very fine wire. Bent in a circle it becomes a wreath, and a wreath looks well round the face of a big wall clock or a grandfather clock. A way of decorating a formal room in the Adam manner was invented by the writer's brother, Rex Whistler. A berry and a leaf of holly are strung alternately on a thread, the needle piercing the leaf at each end to keep it flat. Long chains are then hung round the walls in shallow loops, with short vertical pieces hanging between; or they are tied to circles of wire. To be effective, the whole room should be treated in this manner. Paper decorations were introduced about the middle of the last century or a little later, and are liked by children and best suited to the nursery. If a room is well filled with evergreens it may be thought that no more is wanted than an occasional ball or bell of one colour. When unfolded they have a delightful honeycombed rotundity, and the best are a plain green, red, or orange; for the multicoloured are garish. On the other hand, bought paper-chains that open like a concertina into involved and brilliant shapes are never as charming as those that children make themselves, looping together the little strips of coloured paper that are sold in packets.

Though we no longer decorate the outsides of our houses, the great shops in every city remind us after dark, with their coloured lights and cartouches reflected in the wet mirrors of roadway and pavement, that the gaieties of Christmas are not private. So does a custom recently introduced into England, and already established in some parts of the United States: a large illuminated Christmas tree is placed in the town square or on the village green, and around this centre and symbol of a public festival the carol singers begin or end their peregrination.

Coleridge's German family made a Christmas tree from a bough of yew, but that must surely have been oddly lop-sided, or else the poet was mistaken. The normal tree is of course the fir, and the more symmetrical the better. In preparing it a delicate touch is required and a leisurely hour, but though the tree will be kept a secret from the smaller children, for their elders there is almost as much enjoyment in decking it out as in seeing it alight. In some homes the roots have been covered with moss, and under the lowest branches the Bethlehem scene depicted in miniature, with toy shepherds and their dogs and sheep gathered about the crib, and with match-stick palings stuck with almonds and gilded nuts. Overhead the innumerable pendants, light and bright, the silver and golden bells and shells, balls and stars, the icicles of glass, the twisted red and green candles on every twig, the sweets in silver foil and the toys and manikins that swing beneath them, all these are familiar, if only familiar in recollection to some of us, while the years of austerity forbid the renewal of the lost brilliant and the broken stalactite. And on the apex of the cone there will stand, tiptoe, a being half angel and half fairy, gauze-winged and with a golden crown.

But centuries before any foreigner's tree was lit in this island there were English children at work on the Eve, binding evergreens, fastening little presents, and at last lighting the candles on a device that evoked in them all the pleasure and excitement aroused by the Christmas tree in the Lutherans of Germany. They called it the Kissing Bough or the Kissing Bunch. It did not rise up from the floor in a pyramid of lights: it hung from the ceiling in a luminous crown: a hemisphere of evergreens marked with a ring of candles above, and with a ring of bright red apples below, curiously hinting at fulfilment in the hour of promise. And all this was but the frame to a bunch of mistletoe, suspended a little below the centre to explain the purpose and the name of the device.*

* See also *Notes and Queries*, 5th, 8th, 10th and 11th Series; Robert Holland, *Glossary of Words Used in the County of Chester* (English Dialect Society), 1886, Pt. 2, p. 191; P. H. Ditchfield, *Old English Customs*, 1896, p. 18; the Viscountess Wolseley, *The Countryman's Log-Book*, 1921, p. 304; T. G. Crippen, *Christmas and Christmas Lore*, 1923; Christina Hole, *English Custom and Usage*, 1941, p. 16.

So well liked was the Kissing Bough that it has never been entirely replaced by the tree. There are families in Derbyshire, Cheshire and Staffordshire, in Northumberland, and perhaps in Cornwall and Devon as well, who keep it to this day, and these have given it back to one or two others. Now it is usually a decoration; but we have heard that in Northumberland there are still a few farms and cottages where the presents are hung on the Kissing Bough and the Christmas tree is unknown.

The Bough is not always in the shape of a crown. It may take the form of a completed sphere or globe, rather like the festival lanterns already described, and then the seven apples cluster in the centre of the globe, and the mistletoe hangs in a bunch underneath, where the circles cross. Mistletoe grows well in the West, not so well in the North, where they buy it in large quantities from the gypsies of Herefordshire; so the Kissing Bough did not always hold this provocative bunch, and yet it deserved its name, none the less. In the last century all manner of gay and glittering objects were added to the leaf-hidden frame, as they are to the tree: little robins, rabbits and squirrels, oranges and pears, stiff paper rosettes, bits of tinsel and bright-coloured ribbon, bits of looking-glass, and Bethlehem stars cut out of shiny tin—sometimes the Bethlehem crib, with the dogs and shepherds around it: home-made ornaments most of them; for the delicate icicles and shells that now embellish the Christmas tree were beyond the ken of the farmer's daughters. And then the candles—set in a ring around the middle, or placed here and there about the frame wherever a convenient stalk or twig would hold one.

On Christmas Eve those candles were lit in ceremony, and the Kissing Bough became the visible centre of the festival, lit again on the Day, and every evening thereafter till the Twelve Days were out. It hung from the middle of the ceiling, just high enough from the ground for a couple to stand or stoop and kiss beneath it. Every visitor to the house soon found his way to that point. It was there that the carols were sung in a circle. It was there the Mummers or Guisers held swaggeringly forth, or else, arrived at the final act of their drama, they would all move forward to the Bough to bid farewell. It was indeed the crown and centre of Christmas; and the last kisses of the Eve were under those lights.

Kissing under the mistletoe is said to have been wholly an English custom, only adopted in other lands where the Englishman has taken it. That may not be true, but we are reminded of the fame of England's kisses in late mediæval and Tudor days, already referred to in the Introduction. Man and woman, crony and stranger, they were always kissing one another. The foreign visitor thought it surprising—and rather pleasant, for the beauty of English women was proverbial. Now, we do not embrace so easily in public—quite the reverse in fact—but even to-day no girl is supposed to refuse a kiss when the Golden Bough is above her, and formerly, for every kiss that he took, a young man was entitled to put his hand into the circle of candles and pull off one berry at a time.

It would be interesting to know why the German Tree supplanted the native Bough, or why it caught the imagination when the other was failing to arouse it. We may conclude that it was partly because the Bough had been long since forgotten in the grey, dilated cities, and by the more educated Englishmen everywhere; partly because the Christmas tree shone, as it were, "by Appointment to Her Majesty"; and even more because it ministered to the romantic appetite for *natural* forms; for it was like a tree out of Hans Andersen, a tree from the fairy-tale North where Christmases are always white, and Santa Claus rolls rosy-cheeked between the conifers—a tree living indoors, wonderfully transformed, but still a tree.

That is true. Yet in some parts of the country a fir tree of a good size and shape may be difficult to find, so it is worth remembering that a very delightful, as well as a very ancient, emblem exists, on which the stars and dolls and ribbons may be hung once again as they used to be. It would anyway be pleasant to revive the Kissing Bough, not as an alternative, but simply as a form of decoration, and then the best of all. With its candlelit apples the Bough is in some way typically English, while the tree has never quite ceased, we may think, to appear Teutonic, or at any rate Nordic. In the two customs we recognise the spirit of two peoples, just as we recognise the spirit of England in 'Greensleeves' and the spirit of Scotland in 'The Road to the Isles'.

The framework used to be made of iron or osier, entirely concealed by the evergreens bound closely against it. It can be made just as well, and quite simply, out of pliable wire, and once made the contrivance is good for any number of years.* Only one evergreen should be used on the frame-work, and the most likable are rosemary and box, for these grow narrowly and tightly, look well in candlelight, and give the device a decorative formality. Each apple may be fastened by the stalk to a length of red or blue ribbon, and the Bough itself to a large bow. The two kinds of Bough are shown in the frontispiece; but within the limits of crown and globe there has always been room for inventiveness and many new features may be introduced. Thus, a blue or

* For the 'Globe' type of Bough, five circles of wire should be made, exactly equal. One becomes the 'equator', the other four are the 'meridians'. Eight candles can be set around the 'equator', and another eight inside the globe towards the bottom. Seven red apples, or oranges, form a neat cluster, with one of them in the centre.—See frontispiece.

silver witch-ball may form the centre of the crown, reflecting
the candles at six or eight points and suggesting, together
with the annulus of apples, a model of the solar system,
intended to represent the stations of the sun about the earth
in some pre-Copernican cosmography. Nor is the notion so
far-fetched as it sounds. On the evening of the sun's rebirth
it is likely that the glowing apples once signified nothing
else.

Whether the much larger coloured or decorated lights,
once known as Christmas Candles, are still to be found
among the timeless wares of a single countrified shop, in the
most conservative hamlet of the most unvisited county, is
doubtful. Plain red, green, yellow or orange candles are
common enough, but if a richer and gayer effect is needed, it
is best to buy the long white candles of slow-burning wax
that are for sale in the church shops. Each pair is wound
with ribbon or coloured paper in contrasting spirals, and
these are kept in place by a very small pin pressed into the
wax at top and bottom. One or two pins should be put in a
little way down the spiral, so that when the candle burns
and the ribbon needs to be trimmed from time to time, it
may not altogether untwist itself.

Of an age with the tree in this island is another Victorian
novelty, the Christmas card. Like the Valentine, but fifty
years later, it began as a kind of stationery. In the 'forties,
or even perhaps in the later 'thirties, on notable occasions
like Christmas, the New Year or a birthday, a polite person
might send off a little poem of a sacred or complimentary
character, delicately engraved within a framework of
embossed ornament. Rock & Co. offered a wide range of
examples, and several of these are preserved in the Collection
of Ephemera at Oxford.* One, outside the numbered

* The property of the Oxford University Press.

series, and earlier than the others in technique, bears in Gothic lettering the title—

Christmas Comforts

'Tis the season for friends and relations to meet,
Still closer to link, by the pleasures enjoyed,
Those bonds which endear man to man, making sweet
The life which without them is dreary and void.

This in its regular frame of embossed acanthus, wreaths and vases might to-day be called, without overstraining the name, a Christmas card of a rather formal variety; and though the name was not at that time invented, we ought to regard it as an early example, or at any rate as a progenitor of the custom.

In 1846 a quite authentic Christmas card was published by Summerly's *Home Treasury* office. J. C. Horsley had provided the design, which appeared in colour and took the form of three panels in a rustic framework. In the centre panel there is a homely drinking scene: children, parents and grandparents seated about a table, some of them raising their glasses for a toast. In the panel on either side we have an act of Christmas charity depicted: to the left, "feeding the hungry"; to the right, "clothing the naked." Underneath there appears—for the first time it may be—the now very familiar legend: "A Merry Christmas and a Happy New Year to you."* Horsley claimed in after-years to have been the inventor of the Christmas card, and the claim can be allowed, but only in a limited sense. He may well have designed the first fully pictorial card—that has been disputed, however—but he must have been led to the idea

* Reproduced in *The Studio*, Extra No. Christmas, 1894: also in A. R. Wright, *British Calendar Customs: England*, Vol. III.

by a custom already in existence, the writing of a "Christmas letter" to every acquaintance, on notepaper topped with a poem, or a formal device.

Certainly the immediate future of the Christmas card lay with the ornamental stationers more than with independent artists. No picture cards were printed commercially until 1862, when Messrs. Charles Goodall began to issue designs by G. H. Bennett. After that there was never a year without them. Meanwhile Christmas and New Year notepaper became increasingly popular. So did another form of "stationery"—that was the name for it still in the early 'sixties—the little embossed *cartes de visite*, designed for the same occasions. These began to win special favour for an obvious reason. Families were large, and friends who must be "remembered" were many. Now that Christmas meant more than formerly, now that there was a tree and a row of stockings to prepare for, the writing of a "Christmas letter" twenty times over became something of an imposition. On the *cartes de visite* no more than a name and a greeting were required.

For Christmas, a robin: for New Year's Day, a bunch of Spring flowers.—The emblems appear on both kinds of stationery again and again; and the robin has dominated the Christmas card ever since. There was more than mere fancy in this; for the stationers were continuing an old tradition: the red bird had been long connected with the Christmas season. Like the wren, he had once been sacred: a spark of divinity glimmered in him still.

> The robin and the wren
> Are God Almighty's cock and hen.

Ferocious, yet friendly; man-haunting and still vocal, when

most other birds were timid and mute, he held in his puffed-out breast the very spirit of absent life—of the Summer to be. It was for him, really, that a whole ritual was performed in the apple orchards on Twelfth Night.

The true Christmas card may be said to date from the 1860's, and the influence on it of the old ornamental stationers, then at their prime—Windsor, Sulman, C. & E. Layton, J. T. Wood, and the Paris firm of Marion—was no doubt considerable. At the close of that decade or early in the next, a new kind of card began to appear in the shops. It was much more elaborate than anything seen before, built up out of imported 'scraps' on gilded and lace-edged folders, with 'lift-ups' revealing rhymes, and bunches of holly and mistletoe; the subject being, though by no means invariably sacred, at any rate appropriate to the season. It looked as if the Valentine-makers had broken new territory, and that in fact was the case. Many of these firms were now catering for both festivals—Dean & Sons, for example, and Marcus Ward, who also produced the purely pictorial card—and in their workrooms the Valentine set the pattern that one kind of Christmas card would follow for twenty years. The lace folder or clay surface card did equally well as the basis for either: on that could be imposed the cupids and flowers of the one, or the robins and holly of the other. Then, in the 1880's the 'Valentinian' card—product of so many nimble fingers—disappeared, leaving the field to the individual artist, such as Walter Crane. And a handsome field it was. One firm paid £7,000 in a single year, 1882, for original drawings. But taste was declining, and already the Christmas card had set out on its long road to modern insipidity. Thus do we see it too often on the stationer's counter to-day, wearing out some overworked theme: the robin in the holly as always—but now a stuffed robin, surely?—or the old-world cottage on its knees in the snow, distributing 100-watt candlelight from all its windows.

In search, then, of tolerable cards, the discriminating resort to old prints of flowers, or reproductions of famous paintings, agreeable in themselves but entirely irrelevant to Christmas. That is bad festival manners! There is opportunity here for a publisher to employ a good artist again, who might work with a living poet.* But something original is required, some new departure in material or technique, to put new life in a custom grown flabby, though still very far from expiring.

Revived within living memory, the carols flourish. Yet there are still choirs unfamiliar with 'Lullay my Liking', and the Coventry carol—'Lully, Lullay, thou little tiny child'—which can never, since the reign of Henry VI, have sounded so poignant as when it was sung at Christmas, 1940, about the ruins of Coventry Cathedral. Some of those which are less well known, yet easy to sing, are named in the second part of Appendix B.

Carols exquisitely sung can be heard in many cathedrals during Advent, and in St. Michael's Church, Cornhill; but the most celebrated of carol services, and justly so, is the one which is broadcast each year in the afternoon of Christmas Eve, from King's College Chapel in Cambridge. The procession enters at the West door with candles—the whole building is only candlelit, and therefore obscure. As the service develops, passages from the Gospel story alternate with the nine carols, many of which may have flowered from the same England as the intricate fans of stonework above them, now sensed by the congregation

---

* One or two firms do employ a good artist occasionally, but the cards they produce are seldom appropriate to Christmas.

rather than seen, as the light removes from a midwinter afternoon.

But we associate carols no less with imperfect voices and a humbler environment. The waits were formerly a civic institution; in the words of the Dictionary, "a small body of wind instrumentalists maintained by a city or town at the public charge." They were abolished at the end of the eighteenth century, when it was revealed that they did not justify themselves economically at all. The name was then applied to any parties that sang at front doors about Christmas-time to collect pennies. They are now mostly recruited from the very young, and the musical accomplishment is not great. But fortunately church choirs and other troupes of singers are beginning to travel the streets and lanes with their torches or lanterns, singing for charity—a Victorian custom revived, once common in Devon, for example. The singing is reasonably good, for the singers are well rehearsed, and the songs are of the stuff out of which a Christmas is made; so that money comes easily to a good cause that night. One hopes that the custom will endure, and that repertories will include one or two of the more unfamiliar carols, for there is no better way of re-establishing them.

A party of this kind is improved if the singers can be supported by an instrument. Do the hand-bells sound no longer, with their frangible, star-cold tones ringing out so thinly, after the soft-edged warmth of human voices in harmony? That was a peculiarly Christmas music, but is now seldom to be heard. Instead—but that is no substitute, though appropriate enough—we revive the old custom of pealing the bells of churches on Christmas Eve.

The first age of the carols was also the age of the Nativity play, one item in the great cycles of religious drama that were presented all over the country on open-air stages or

c

'pageants'. In a later England, when the secular drama had superseded the religious, Christmas became in London pre-eminently the season of the masque, just as to-day it is the season of the pantomime. With Ben Jonson to write the words for them, Inigo Jones to design the dresses, and members of the Royal Family taking part, the masques of the Stuart court became too popular; it was necessary to indicate to certain noblemen that they were needed on their own estates, making Christmas for their tenants and servants. Now after the lapse of centuries we are returning to the older idea of a Christmas entertainment, to the Nativity play, revived in village hall and church and schoolroom. Few of us regard the impersonating of the Mother and the Child as idolatrous, and we do not need to be Roman Catholics, High Churchmen, or even churchmen at all, to sense the beauty of the Gospel story enacted by the young. Some of the young men and women who took part in the elaborate Nativity play at Springhead before the war* were not, we suspect, very orthodox members of any recognisable church, but they moved in the story and sang the carols that are the property of us all.

Dramatic effects are more in favour than they have been since the death of Archbishop Laud. Entering at the West end of a church in Christmas week we are likely to encounter a Crib, and round about it figures of the Virgin Mary, Joseph, and the shepherds, arranged in adoration; a custom made popular by St. Francis, always kept in the Roman Church, and recently revived in the Church of England. On the Eve of Epiphany the cradle and its backcloth may be changed, and the shepherds replaced by the Three Kings. The Crib is delightful in theory, depressing in practice, so

* Described by Rolf Gardiner in *England Herself*, pp. 143-4, and revived in 1946.

poor a sentiment is generally displayed. Indeed, contemplating the insipidities relished by certain High Anglican and Roman Catholic priests, the church-shop gadgets and vapid pictures with which they dado their churches, up to a tide-mark of sentimentality, one is driven to speculate whether the best guardian of good architecture is not, after all, the Evangelical parson who leaves it alone. But that is by the way. A still newer experience in Christmas week is to enter a cathedral at nightfall, and discover, as we can in most cathedrals and many churches at the present time, a very large Christmas tree coruscating in the shadows of the nave. At the foot of the tree there is a mound of toys: children have placed them there anonymously, and presently they will be given away to the hospitals. The silver balls among the branches are of the girth of witch-balls and the lights upon them, burning red and blue, are only electric bulbs; and yet there is buoyancy and mystery here, in the darkness of the church, a kind of intent and gleaming charity. The two trees at St. Paul's, one at the West end of the nave, and one outside in the portico, are brought each year from the King's estate at Sandringham. In any cathedral the decorations must be large and conspicuous and therefore for reasons of economy few, while in a classical cathedral they need to be formal. One can imagine a device hung from the Whispering Gallery on wires; an immense crown of lights and formal evergreens.

With the Christmas tree now established in church, a novelty of the 1930's, there is justification for describing a service recently given by Spain to America. It takes place on Christmas Eve, and resembles Tenebræ in reverse. At the beginning, all lights are extinguished except for one pair of candles. In the darkness the shape of a Christmas tree can be discerned, standing in view of the congregation. The psalm

'Out of the deep' is sung, followed by the first of the Messianic prophecies; and as the voice utters it a candle is lit on the tree. Another voice tells of another prophecy, and a second candle shines out. Then the Gospel narrative is read, each passage followed by a carol, a child's voice rising solo, the choir responding, and all the while new points of flame are appearing about the tree, until at last, with the words "I am the Light of the World", every bough is alight. This is the height of dramatic representation (a height, however, at which members of the Roman Church breathe easily), and there are some who would be distracted by so much display. Would not St. Paul declare it to be a matter of temperament, over which we can exercise a mutual charity? In this way, at all events, do some Christians make use of sight and hearing, and doubtless of smell, all at once, three of the five senses which Blake declared to be "the chief inlets of Soul in this age".

CHRISTMAS DAY

DECEMBER 25TH

Some say that ever 'gainst that season comes
Wherein our Saviour's birth is celebrated
The bird of dawning singeth all night long,
And then, they say, no spirit dare stir abroad,
The nights are wholesome; then no planets strike,
No fairy takes, nor witch hath power to charm,
So hallowed and so gracious is the time.

WILLIAM SHAKESPEARE—*Hamlet*

FOR full members of the Church the day begins at dawn or midnight with the sacrament. The midnight mass wins favour from two causes, it would seem, characteristic of the period we live in: a new taste for the dramatic in worship; and, more humbly, domestic convenience; for where there are children and no servants, husband and wife may be unable to communicate at any other time. The hour was first chosen at Rome in the fifth century to symbolise the idea that Christ is born at midnight—a mystical idea in no way affected by historical evidence, or rather, by the lack of it; for neither the hour nor the day of the event is known. At first there was some variety of opinion among the Churches, and it was only in the fourth century that Western Europe as a whole adopted December 25th.

For children the day begins with a weight on the toes, long, angular, and many-faceted as a leg by Picasso. The stocking should be opened by candlelight: no other light is resonant at that high frequency of excitement. To be decently traditional it should contain, at the top, an apple; at the toe an orange; and somewhere in between, among the many objects done up in foil or coloured paper, a new silver sixpence. The cornucopia spills slowly, and yet before long will be rousing the house to a thin music of whistles and trumpetings.

But these are the merest *hors d'œuvres*. The real presents have yet to be given, and in our country there has never been general agreement on the hour for this. One can only say that for nearly a century they have not been given by hand, but wrapped in gay paper, inscribed and arranged in a heap for each member of the household, and none should be absent when the moment comes to undo them.

Wherever the open fireplace exists—and there will always be some who prefer the living flame to a meaningless panel in the wall—the Christmas log might be remembered, not because of its antiquity (many ancient customs are quite unfitted for survival) but because it demonstrates in a particular way that time progresses in a twelve-month spiral, with the Christmas before and the Christmas to follow as the points in the spiral immediately below and above us,

The log will be chosen and cut beforehand. Ash is the proper tree: ash that burns green, and was therefore sacred to the sun on whose birthday nature was reborn: ash that is said in Devon to have warmed the Child Jesus at his earliest bath: ash that was believed in Scandinavia to be the wood of the world-tree, Yggdrasil, with its roots knotted in Hell and its boughs supporting Heaven. The log was large, and must now, of necessity, be small. Perhaps the 'ashen faggot' of Devon is more suited to survival. In that county a bundle of ash sticks were bound together with nine ash-bands on Christmas Eve, and brought in on the Day with much rejoicing.* No less ceremony attended the bringing in of the log in other parts of the island. Sometimes it would be sprinkled with corn and cider, and sometimes it would be dragged in with a girl enthroned upon it, and then there would be glasses raised to her health. In any event, a new fire would be made, and the log kindled with the last fragment of the previous log, kept throughout the year for this purpose—a rule that was no pretty fancy, but a profound recognition of continuity. By the time dinner was brought in the symbolic brand would be ablaze.

Christmas dinner has always been a great occasion, indeed the principal meal of the year; and thus it remains. Rank divided the people of England in former times much less unalterably than class divides them to-day, when all are supposed to be equal. Rank could forget itself on occasion: snobbery never relents. Perhaps, after all, it is better to be called an inferior and loved than to be called an equal and despised; but that is a notion that sticks in the gullet of this age. Enough to record that on Christmas Day master and servant sat down in the great hall to banquet together in genuine though brief equality. The Romans at the Saturnalia had done the same, and the Scandinavians at Yule, but in Christian England it was done in a better spirit, in the spirit of man's joy in the Nativity, that act of divine condescension before which all men are indeed equal. St. Francis of Assisi maintained that even the animals ought to share in our joy, however dimly and simply. Thus he explained and christened an ancient observance, whereby it was common,

* Or perhaps more frequently on the Eve itself; but the tendency for some time has been to transfer all customs from the Eve to the Day.

in this country among others, to give extra food to the cattle and dogs on Christmas morning, and to fix a sheaf of corn to the roof, where of course it attracted a cloud of delighted birds, especially in a white Christmas or a very hard one.

In great houses the main dish was the boar's head, once eaten in honour of the "golden-bristled sun-boar", still garnished with rosemary and bays for the summer returning, and still with its mouth propped open on a solar apple or orange. And so it appears to this day in the Queen's College at Oxford, brought in with a macaronic carol.*

> The Boar's Head in hand bear I,
> Bedecked with bays and rosemary;
> I pray you my masters be merry,
>   *Quod estis in convivio.*

But the dish is too gross and too splendid for the century of the kitchenette, and it has gone with plum porridge and frumenty and with that colossal envelope of pabulum, the Christmas pie. In those great houses there was a time when turkey was unknown and goose would be thought very humble fare. At Nonsuch or Hampton Court it would be roasted swans, peacocks or bustards that sailed out of the kitchens at Christmas, dressed again in their beauty, spread wings and tails, and with gilded beaks, or with beaks nipped on a sponge of blazing spirit. But the phœnix was not for common palates. It would be the goose that appeared on most tables, the traditional meat of the festival, remembered in the rhyme. The turkey was imported from Mexico, where it was discovered by the European invaders in a domestic state, and it arrived in this country about the year 1542. Presently it began to replace the nobler birds, and later, but much more slowly, and never completely, the goose.

* While the restrictions of war remain in force, a *papier mâché* head is used

Before the end of the eighteenth century, according to Hone,* Norwich alone was sending to London nearly 1,000 Christmas turkeys in a single day.

Mince pies were already popular in Shakespeare's England —popular and varied. There were pies of minced chicken, of neats' tongues, and of eggs, in addition to the pies for which alone we now reserve the name, full of spiced raisins, remotely allusive to Epiphany and the gifts of the three kings. Raisins and spices were also, together with breadcrumbs, wine and fruit juice, the main ingredients of plum porridge, a concoction that does not seem to have hardened into a pudding before the year 1670. No doubt the customs of the pudding are those of the porridge perpetuated. Every member of the household takes a hand in the stirring and secretly wishes a wish. A silver coin (formerly a threepenny bit), a ring and a thimble are stirred in, the coin to bring fortune to the finder, the ring a wedding, and the thimble a life of single blessedness. On the Day, a sprig of the reddest holly is stuck in the top of the pudding, and then brandy may be heated above a candle, lit, and poured over it in a river of fire. After dark, there is Snapdragon, when the lights are put out and raisins are snatched between finger and thumb from a flat dish of flaring brandy. When none are left, salt is thrown in and the flame expires with a green glance.

Tangerines, dates, chocolates, almonds and raisins, any sort of nuts, including roast chestnuts, crystallised fruit and ginger are all in the Christmas bill of fare, and none of these has been added recently. Of drink there is less that can be said, except that it is the night for a rum punch or other hot drink, passed from hand to hand as a loving-cup and sipped while the chestnuts are popping. But 'lamb's wool' is out:

* *The Every-Day Book,* Col. 1606.

the steaming syrup into which Shakespeare heard "the roasted crabs hiss", when they dropped one after another. To make it—but we shall hardly attempt so much in 1947— we must, according to a recipe from the Royal kitchen of 1633,* "Boil three pints of ale; beat six eggs, the whites and yolks together; set both to the fire in a pewter pot; add roasted apples, sugar, beaten nutmegs, cloves and ginger; and, being well brewed, drink it while hot."

When darkness falls the candles are lit on the Kissing Bough, and beneath this floating crown of a proffered happiness—a crown of fruits and lights, formal as Ariadne's in the Titian picture, or as its original in the Summer sky itself—the children may begin their party. There will be a cake with "A Merry Christmas" for motto; a cake once again geologically sound, with one stratum of icing, and one of marzipan, the whole superimposed on alluvial darkness. There will be red paper crackers by each plate. There will be arms crossed, forming a circle to pull them; and there will be in reward the tin whistle and the flimsy cap of bright-coloured paper, opening into helmet or bonnet or bird. Even so did the Roman Briton put on a fantastic headpiece for the Saturnalia, and the islanders have not forgotten; before the days of paper caps in crackers—and they are recent—the Lord of Misrule was ordering crowns and coxcombs. Evergreen garlands were also very much in use. They are still used in some families to honour a Winter birthday, and they are not difficult to contrive.† One might be worn by each child at a Christmas party.

Candles and cakes, games and garlands are very old: to these joys the modern world adds little but indoor fireworks. These are of three kinds: bright lights, loud bangs, and

---

* T. G. Crippen, *Christmas and Christmas Lore*, 1923, p. 101.
† See p. 228.

creeping cinders of one kind or another. There are 'sparklers' that grow, beneath finger and thumb, from little stabs of flame to irregular snatches of golden, twig-like sparks—build up into a Christmas tree of light—and decline at last into a single, ardent drop. There is the 'joke-bomb', loudly sprinkling the room with whistles and very weak rhymes. There is the paper 'fern' curling and uncurling dimly and patiently downward. And then there is the 'serpent's egg', out of which, as if by magic out of the plate itself, there begins to be ejaculated, with the lightness of a feather and yet with considerable firmness, spasmodically though, as if birth were a difficult matter—and indeed it is often arrested half-way—the serpent.

At last there is the tree, radiant for the second evening, or, as it may be, for the first—since the Eve appears to be losing the custom and the Day to be acquiring it, a development of which Prince Albert would surely disapprove, gratified though he would be to look into our houses and see how many of us are in his debt. Suppose, then, it has been reserved for this evening, decorated and kept behind locked doors for this hour. When the children enter that room it is already alight, and all other lights are extinguished; found there like a presence already arrived and serenely awaiting them, patient in splendour; becalming at first, or almost hypnotic; it needs only to be looked at. Even to older eyes it seems to be more than it is, more than a conifer covered with objects of meal and glass and wax, this image of a tree whose buds are flames, flowering at midwinter, a tree burning and unconsumed, evocative of the flourishing bay tree, and the burning bush, of the mystical 'Dream of the Rood', the Tree of Calvary itself, whose shadow is faint but indelible across the lights of the Nativity.

At a slight draught from the window the candles flow one

way together, with a glance whose transcendental drift we are never quite in time to gather. Presently a twig, too near a flame, cracks in the heat, shrivels to the foot of a bird, and utters its one cry of fragrance.

BOXING DAY

DECEMBER 26TH

*"Reaching all back long before Oliver Grumble's time—to the
days of the Pagan Turks."*
John Durbeyfield in *Tess of the D'Urbervilles.*
THOMAS HARDY

THIS day is the Feast of Stephen, the first man to be
martyred for believing in Christ. The origin of the more
popular name is undetermined. Some hold that it alludes
to the church alms-box which used to be opened on Boxing
Day and the contents given to the poor; others, with greater
likelihood, to the earthenware box that the young apprentice
brought to the door of each of his master's clients; and it is
still customary to give a 'Christmas box' on this day rather
than another. The parson would be dispatching to the pauper
bread, cheese and beer; a gentleman, compelled to go a
journey, would find that the innkeeper charged him less for
his dinner; and when preparing her Christmas food, the
goose or turkey, plum puddings and pies, the farmer's wife
would have set apart a very large pie to be cut up this morning
and distributed to the labourers' families. For on Christmas
Day right-minded citizens showed good will to members of
their own household; but on Boxing Day to a wider circle.

So passed by the first of the Twelve Days of Christmas,
with the plough under thatch and the shutters up in the
workshop window, while the gentry entertained the
farmers, and the farmers entertained their men. In

eighteenth century Cumberland, during this period, the farmers would be meeting night after night in a different house, every man host in his turn, to sing and play, drink punch and eat good food; and should there come a knock at the door, the stranger, benighted on the fells and drawn to their promising lights, would find there a northerner's welcome.

But to the modern child Boxing Day is often an anti-climax; more so than to earlier children for whom Christmas can have been neither so conspicuous in the calendar nor so magical in itself. It is best to keep something in hand for these sober hours, a few presents still to be opened, a party with a conjuror or a Punch and Judy, or better, a pantomime or a play: a Christmas masque, it may be, performed by the children themselves. Until quite recently Boxing Day was notable in the theatre as the beginning of the pantomime season. Children in the big towns would ask one another which of the favourites they were going to see. Yet, though a character known as 'pantomimus' performed in dumb show for the ancient Romans, the pantomime intended, or partly intended, for children is not very old. Before it developed, the Augustan theatre-manager would present, on this evening, what might be called an Augustan 'morality play'—'George Barnwell' was perhaps the most celebrated—for the edification of the London 'prentices. It resembled the earlier 'morality' about as closely as an eighteenth century Protestant resembled a fifteenth century Catholic, its object being the same, to edify by entertaining. The moral play was well attended, and in the second half of the century the managers began to extend the scope of the pantomime, newly established in England, by inviting the children who were recently home from school to witness a fairy tale with a harlequinade at the end. And so it was that the ancient mythology of Harlequin and Columbine, Clown and Pantaloon adapted itself to a modern audience composed partly of children, and in so doing, it must be admitted, lost much of its quality. Topical songs and other extraneous 'turns' crept in, while the advance in Victorian stagecraft made possible, and then indispensable, the breath-taking climax of the transformation scene. To-day the pantomime is little better than a *revue*, displaying certain conventional features, inherited from a distant past. With one company competing against another, the season begins early. By the end of it, most of the favourites will have appeared in London or the Provinces: 'Cinderella' and 'The Sleeping Beauty', 'Dick Whittington and his Cat,' 'Aladdin' and 'Robinson Crusoe,' 'The Babes in the Wood,' 'Jack and the Beanstalk' and 'Mother Goose' Much of the fun is quite above, or below, the comprehension of children, but a "real children's pantomime" is generally advertised among the rest. It will take more than the wit and vulgarity of Walt Disney to tarnish those tinsel splendours.

Certainly Christmas does all in his power to compensate the little townsman for his dirty snow and shop-soiled holly. Pantomimes are not for the country child. And yet even in the world of the theatre, a world of exalted mystery to children however humble its aspect, the latter would sometimes have the advantage, if antiquity were the only criterion in drama. For it is still possible in several counties to command a visit from a theatrical company whose singular stock-in-trade is incomparably the oldest dramatic entertainment in England, quite outclassing in this respect the sacred drama of the Middle Ages, and, what is more, exhibiting an unbroken sequence of performances, year by year, through at least eight centuries. We are speaking, of course, of the Mummers' Play. To assert that the sequence has never been broken would be rash, if it were not obvious that it never can have been, at any rate before the present century. For the words were not written down, and the actors were, and still are, ordinary countrymen meeting together after work, or on festival evenings, to give a performance. They learnt by word of mouth, and in such a way that each new recruit to the company would assume one character, and receive from his predecessor, retiring, only the lines and cues of one part. In origin the play was at least as remote from Shakespeare as Shakespeare is remote from ourselves: rather as the shape of the violin retains the imprint of the Baroque age in which it was perfected, the Mummers' Play evokes the England of the Crusades in which it received its present form, (though English history has provided additional themes from time to time, such as the death of Nelson, still honoured by the Quidhampton Mummers of Wiltshire in their epilogue). Beyond that, no one can say to what masquerade of the Saturnalia, and beyond that again to what vanishing point in human antiquity, it returns.

At the end of so long and obscure a descent it is not surprising that a Cheshire 'text' and a Wiltshire 'text', once they are written down and compared, should be found to differ, but rather that they should resemble each other so closely. The main characters are ubiquitous. There is Father Christmas (for this is notably a Christmas entertainment), King George (formerly the Saint), Bold Slasher or Turkey Snipe (originally the Turkish Knight), Quack Doctor, Twing-Twang or Little Johnny Jack (who is Robin Hood), Rumour and sometimes Lawyer and Valiant Soldier. The costumes are curious, and remarkably like those of an African medicine-man: dresses sewn all over with strips of cloth; high headdresses so thickly hung with streamers that the face beneath is entirely concealed. The plot is equally childish and mysterious. St. George—or, as he may have become since the eighteenth century, King George—is confronted with the Turkish Knight:

> In comes I the Turkey Snipe,
> Come from my Turkish Land to fight.

He challenges the infidel and kills him, and is thereupon stricken with peculiar remorse. "Oh!" cries George,

> Only behold and see what I have been and done,
> Cut and slain my brother just like the evening sun!

The Doctor is summoned and appears instantly. He is a widely travelled man, and lets us know it. "I've travelled India, South India and Bendigo," he announces, and sometimes he will also lay claim to having visited "Itty-Titty, where there's neither wall nor city". Then, which is perhaps more to the point in the present emergency, he tell us,

> I carry a little bottle by my side
> Which is called the Oppliss Poppliss Drops.

These he administers to the dead man, who revives at once, and all is well.*

Beneath the modern mummery of Christian knight and infidel—for here we must think of the Crusades as modern history—we can discern the actions of a man impersonating the Slain God at the Winter Solstice and the Vernal Equinox,

* For other accounts of the Mummers' Play, in its several versions, see Iolo A. Williams, *English Folk-Song and Dance*, 1935; Edith Olivier, *Country Moods and Tenses*, 1941; George Long, *The Folklore Calendar*, 1930; P. Crawford, *In England Still*, 1938.

that is to say, at Christmas and Easter, still the principal seasons of the Mummers' Play. Yet in spite of the charm and the extraordinary interest of this drama, handed down piecemeal by one rustic to another, so that many of the words have long since become gibberish, in spite of its recent revival in at least twelve villages, after reaching a state very close to extinction, it is questionable if the Mummers' Play can be regarded as a living, or at any rate as a lively, custom at all. If it survives it will be under new conditions, preserved by the educated as a curiosity, a dramatic monument or a picturesque antique. Clearly it will mean no more than that to the countryman who reads the newspaper and goes to the cinema. What magic lurks in Itty-Titty for an audience that has studied the world in hemispheres?—Penicillin has drained the virtue from the Oppliss Poppliss Drops.

NEW YEAR'S DAY

JANUARY 1ST

*To the past we can do nothing, we can only remember it with
reverence and gratitude, or with remorse and indignation. The
future may bring with it the realisation of our desires, hopes and
dreams. But it also inspires us with terror.*

N. BERDYAEV—*The Destiny of Man*

"A HAPPY New Year" was a greeting in ancient Rome, and
the wealthier Romans would provide their friends with
baskets of dates and figs, garnished with gold leaf.
No doubt the Roman Britons had a similar custom, and
since it is known to have been Anglo-Saxon as well, we may
say that the New Year present and the New Year greeting
have been with us throughout the greater part of our history.
The Elizabethan courtier gave handsomely to his Queen on
this day, and in Ben Jonson's masque of Christmas, already
mentioned, there is a character described as "New-year's-
gift, with an orange, and a sprig of rosemary gilt on his head,
his hat full of brooches, with a collar of gingerbread". The
orange was a favourite present, generally stuck with cloves
in the form of a pomander. But in the last century the
New Year declined while Christmas revived—the two
festivals compete and are never equally robust in any one
country—and in 1862 Chambers observed that the presents
were no longer given except to children. To-day, they are
seldom given at all in the South. In Scotland, of course,
where the reformers managed to get rid of Christmas, the
New Year is boisterously kept, and in Northumberland too

there are shopkeepers at work on Christmas Day who never fail to put up their shutters a week afterwards. Now the South begins to imitate the North. The tendency is to herd together for vague amusement in public places. The steps of St. Paul's are crowded with 'community singers', and the London hotels with dancers and diners in convivial mood.

The Church had attempted in the fifth century to baptise the festival by renaming it the Feast of the Circumcision; but perhaps the Gentiles of the North were not greatly stirred by that event. The customs of the day, once pagan, are now secular: and thus, unredeemed, the final minutes of December 31st are somewhat sobering to a thoughtful person. Behind him there extends a length of time, unfavourable perhaps, but at any rate accepted, secure beyond alteration. In front, and approaching at the rate of sixty seconds to the minute, is an equal period, offering almost unlimited scope to misfortune. What trials may have been endured when the bell tolls for another year? Certainly the moment is big with meaning; but the meaning is merely that time passes, life wears out: not, as a rule a rejoicing idea. The instinct of Wesley and his friends was therefore sound in attempting to turn the night into a "watch night", with a short service at twelve o'clock and a specially-written hymn, "Come let us anew our journey pursue." In a few parishes the 'old hundredth' or another psalm is sung on the tower top. Yet on a festival we like to be festive, and the world growing older by a year is no great reason for festivity. We can choose to be sociable and gay for the sake of gaiety, which is good enough; or we can choose to be private and pensive. But the gaiety and the meaning will not be closely allied, as they are outstandingly at Christmas.

There is, or there should be, a note of solemnity or even a

hint of apprehension in the New Year ceremony known as "first footing", a ceremony of the North of England which has come South in the last two hundred years; and perhaps even more a ceremony of Scotland—very popular there since the abolition of Christmas. The household is gathered in one room awaiting the stroke of midnight in silence. As the chime dies away a loud knock at the front door is heard. Opened, it reveals a stranger, a strange man it should be, and one with dark hair.* No one greets him, yet he enters without a word, and it is seen that he holds a branch in one hand and a sprig of mistletoe in the other. He walks to the fire, puts the branch on the flames and the sprig on the mantelpiece. Then he turns and wishes the company a happy New Year; silence is broken, and he is given a glass of wine and a slice of Christmas cake by the master of the house. But the ritual has many variants. Sometimes, instead of a branch and a twig, he brings in bread, salt and coal, ancient symbols of life, hospitality and warmth. Sometimes he is offered a new silver coin along with the cake and the wine. Sometimes he carries the mistletoe about and makes good use of its properties.

The symbol is not hard to explain. He is the new-born year, and therefore strange and a little awe-inspiring, as the dark-haired primitive Iberians must have seemed to the fair-haired conquerors: his knock must be answered at once, for he enters by right and without invitation. He may also be the new-born sun, for he brings the emblem of heat in one hand; and the new-born Spring, if he holds in the others a twig of undying green. He is respectfully attended, for his good will is desired.

A young man will wait at the door of his sweetheart for the stroke of twelve. A night-walker may be suborned in the

* This ruling is not universal. In some towns he has to be fair.

THE NEW YEAR ENTERS

'First Footing' at midnight with a branch and a twig mistletoe. *Drawn by Robin Jaques.*

street. Often, in the North, a dark-haired man has performed the office at several houses in turn. Failing a
stranger, a member of the household may appear at the door,
masked, and perhaps in a costume embroidered with evergreens, after the fashion of May Day's 'Jack-in-Green'. In a
modern version of the ritual, much less dramatic, the whole
party goes out into the old year just before midnight, and the
youngest member is the first to cross the threshold, representing the unknown spirit.*

The dying year should be tolled out on the church bells,
and the new-born infant welcomed with a peal—a custom
greatly revived in the 1930's—; while at the same moment
the sirens are clamorous in the ports. During the eighteenth
century, when 'first footing' was hardly known in the South
of England, glasses were raised at a quarter to twelve to "the
Old Friend—Farewell! Farewell! Farewell!", and then at
midnight to "the New Infant" with three "Hip-hip-hoorahs!"
From a much older England we derive the custom of
dancing-in the New Year to which Scotland has now added
the refinement of Auld Lang Syne, that heartbreaking dirge
of the lachrymose. It would have been better if we had
adopted the midnight flourish of trumpets introduced by
the Prince Consort in 1841; but trumpeters are hard to
come by. That year the Queen heard them at Windsor.
The trumpets, she observed, "had a fine solemn effect which
quite affected dear Albert, who turned pale, and had tears
in his eyes, and pressed my hand very warmly."

* It was formerly a custom for the company to go out *after* midnight to wish
all living things on the property good luck, and then triangular mince pies,
known as 'God-cakes', would be eaten in honour of the Trinity.

TWELFTH DAY

*Gallantry seemed to have taken it up, when Superstition had
been compelled to let it fall.*

HENRY BOURNE—*Antiquitates Vulgares*

As the Manifestation of Christ to the Gentiles, the first
proof that He was not born to be King of the Jews only,
Epiphany has always been treasured with special warmth by
the peoples of Europe, and the Three Kings honoured as our
earliest representatives. Epiphany marks the end of the
twelve days of Christmas, and in the reign of George IV it
was very well kept, especially in London. The children were
out all day, patrolling the streets in bands and playing curious
tricks on the passers-by. Then, as daylight faded, certain
windows were seen to be shining with unusual brilliance.
They were the pastrycooks' windows, and closer inspection
revealed that the brilliance emanated from an immense
number of candles, supplemented, in the most modern
shops, by the "famed gas lights" that were London's latest
enchantment. Embowered in holly and ivy, these lights
were doubled and redoubled, thrown back and forth by
sheets of looking-glass, set one way and another and
festooned in artificial flowers. Already a small crowd was
collecting in front of each window and the scene within
was worth pausing a moment to look at, on the journey
home or to a Twelfth Night celebration. Each window was
the frame to an ephiphany of icing sugar. Each shop was

entirely filled, on this night, with Twelfth Cakes, large and small, garnished with "stars, castles and kings, dragons, palaces and churches, and with innumerable other forms in snow-white confectionery, painted with variegated colours and glittering by excess of light from the mirrors".

But the brightness faded as the century grew older. Chambers observed that the confectioner's window no longer glistened in 1864 as it had in his youth. Yet *The Graphic* of March, 1870, declared that Twelfth Cakes continued to be made for a great many houses. That is hardly true of the present time; for the Twelfth is no longer a holiday. But it is still a festival; at a children's party on this evening the customs of the day could be pleasantly revived. An iced cake there would have to be, even if not as rich and dark as in earlier years, "dark with citron and plums and heavy as gold"; even though we should lack the art and the means to bring it to the table "studded all over with glittering flowers, like ice-plants, and red and green knots of sweetmeat, and hollow yellow crusted crowns, and kings and queens".*

It is indeed the evening for Royalty and their regalia. First the King and Queen must be discovered, acclaimed and crowned. That may be a custom derived from a primitive age, when a mock-king was enthroned and afterwards sacrificed to the god of fertility. The sacrifice vanished, but the festival kept its monarch, and in time he became associated with the Epiphany Kings. In Rome he was chosen by lot, and in the lottery beans were used. In England there are three ways of electing him, of which one is clearly the original. A bean and a pea are put in the cake, and when it is cut and distributed he who finds the bean is King and she who finds the pea is Queen. If the bean is found by a girl

* William Hone, *The Every-Day Book*, Vol. I, Col. 52.

she must name her sovereign, and if the pea by a man, he has the pleasure of choosing his consort and proclaiming an attachment before the company. Alternatively, bean and pea are replaced by two silver coins, a shilling and a sixpence, for example. If the third method is adopted, not only a King and Queen will be chosen, but an entire court or government, and this is perhaps the best suited to a children's party, since everyone present will be provided with a character, which he is supposed to remember throughout the evening. The characters may be real or fictitious personages. On the masculine side they might include the Prince of Wales, if there were a Prince of Wales, the Lord Chamberlain, the Prime Minister, the Archbishop of Canterbury; on the feminine, the Queen Mother, the Princess Royal, Maids of Honour and Ladies in Waiting. In the last century there were picture cards for sale illustrating such characters, and others more fanciful. To-day they should be written on strips of paper, each with a rhyme or picture if possible, folded over and placed in two bowls for the lottery, according to sex. Two golden crowns are waiting on the table.

On this night the Christmas decorations come down, in token that the Twelve Days are at an end. In earlier centuries, when the Christmas holiday lasted through the whole of January, the evergreens were renewed from time to time and not taken down till Candlemas; and that is what Herrick recommends. But for the past three hundred years it has been the more general practice to remove them on Twelfth Night. The leaves are crisp and shrivelled by now and fit for the timely bonfire, the burning of Christmas. Burn they will, especially the tree if it has died, the spectres of all its needles funnelled up into the air and descending again in grey-white ashes, slower than snow.

But if the tree is alive, to-morrow it must return in humble green to the wood.

To this night, also, there belongs a remarkably complete example of primitive ritual, kept up here and there in the present age, though now largely as a frolic. Less than a century ago it was still common practice in the cider counties of the west, and a part of the evening's entertainment.* The men and women of the farm went out into the orchard after dark, the men armed with shotguns and lanterns, and one of them carrying a pail of cider into which roasted apples had been broken. This he put down in the middle of the trees. Each man in turn then dipped a cup in the pail, walked to one of the trees, drank, threw the rest of it over the roots, and placed in a fork of the branches a morsel of cake soaked in cider "for the robin". The company then gathered about the tree to sing the Wassailing Song, while the men, raising their guns together, peppered the leafless boughs with shot. Guns are not many centuries old. We can imagine them, before the ritual was 'modernised' in this manner, hurling handfuls of stones into the branches, or banging sticks on buckets to stir up the drowsy spirit. Everything was done to encourage him by mimicry, and to ensure a good crop by willing it. In some orchards the tips of the lowest branches were pulled down till they reached the cider in the pail. In others the whole company stooped to the earth three times about the tree, rose slowly with the gestures of a man shouldering a sack stuffed full of apples, and concluded with a shout of triumph and a blast on the horn. It was no mere frolic originally. The laughter in the orchard has grown more jocular with the centuries.

"Wes hál!", that is to say, "Be in good health! Be fortunate!", were the usual words of a toast in Saxon England,

* The Illustrated London News, Jan. 12th, 1860.

[79]

to which the rejoinder was "Drinc hál!" In Middle English they had become "Waes hail", and now, in the song, "What sale"—long since a meaningless phrase to the countryman. Not that there is only on record a single version of the song. There are at least thirty, and here is one of them:

What sale, what sale in our town.
The cup is white but the ale is brown,
The cup is made of the best of clay,
Come, pretty old fellow, I'll drink to thea.

I hope your trees will bear and bow
Apples and pears and plums, I do vow,
Hats full, caps full, three bushel bags full,
All under the trees, hooray, hooray!
(And a little heap under the stairs.)

It would be tempting to speculate on the lost significance of a few of these lines. "Town" here is evidently "tun", still possessed of its original meaning, an enclosure or farm. The "pretty old fellow" was once, surely, the spirit of the trees, rather than their owner. Next dawn the bird will peck at the sodden cake that the cycle of cider may be renewed. And what more fitting sanctuary for the warm spirit of life in Winter than the robin's unique jot of flame, that cinder dandled by the wind in numb branches?

PLOUGH SUNDAY AND PLOUGH MONDAY

THE FIRST AFTER TWELFTH DAY

The land is lonely now: Anathema.
R. S. HAWKER—*The Quest of the Sangreal*

ON Plough Monday work was resumed on the farm, emblematically at least, for no serious work was attempted till Tuesday, such was the festive character of this day.* In many parishes the young labourer was up and dressing a long while before daylight, and so were the girls of the farm, for if he could get his plough staff, hatchet or whip beside the fireplace before the kettle was on, he secured the promise of a cock at Shrovetide. Presently twenty or thirty young men from the outlying farms were to be seen gathering at the entrance of the village, conspicuously dressed. Jackets had been left behind, and the men appeared in clean white shirts, embellished at arm and shoulder with large, bright-coloured bows and knots of ribbon, and with ribbons about their hats. Among them were two figures still more out-landishly got up. One was the Bess or Betsy, a boy masquerading as a woman, with a tall hat and false nose; the other the Fool, dressed in skins like a Bacchanal, and armed with a bladder. The remainder began to form up in file, each rank paying out a rope that was fastened to a plough— a wooden plough as well scrubbed and beribboned as them-selves. Then the leader took hold of the stilts, and the

* See William Hone, *The Every-Day Book*, Vol. I, Col. 71.

procession moved off. Horns were blown, or the fiddle and drum struck up. The Fool ran in and out among the spectators, the pennies rattled in the Betsy's box. They drove the plough to the centre of the village and there a circle was formed and the sword dancers stepped out. They were well trained in their lilting choreography, and the dance they danced—North Country miners dance it still— was clearly derived like the Mummers' Play from a pre- historic fertility rite. In the Betsy we see a last caricature of Freyia, the Venus of the North, whom the Old Saxons adored in Holstein before the invasion;* while in the dance itself we see the beheading of a man. Ritual murder has left its mark, clearly or faintly, on many of our festivals. But there is no evidence at all that it ever took place in this country after the Roman conquest. This would imply that the Nordic peoples, from whom we are largely descended, had already abandoned the fact for the fiction before they settled in the land. If that is so, the mimicry in the Sword Dance and the Harvest field must be ancient indeed.

Now the circling dancers approach their climax, and suddenly the Fool kneels in their midst. The swords, locked together, are lowered over his head. Gripping them still, the dancers whirl about him: with a shout the lock is broken: and the Fool falls dead.

The Revesby Play of Lincolnshire resembles the dance even more closely than the Mummers', for there it is the Fool's five sons who cut him down with their swords.

> Good people all, you see what we have done;
> We have cut down our father like the evening sun,
> And here he lies all in his purple gore,
> And we are afraid he will never dance more.

* H. M. Chadwick, *The Origin of the English Nation*, 1907, chap. X.

But the fellow struggles to his knees without a trace of ill-feeling:

> No, no, my children; by chance you are all mista'en,
> For here I find myself, I am not slain:
> But I will rise, your sport for to advance,
> And with you all, brave boys, I'll have a dance.*

In the Middle Ages part of the money in the Betsy's box provided for the Plough Light, a lamp kept burning throughout the year before an image in the church, and never allowed to go out. If it did go out, dark days were prophesied: a superstition the reformers were glad to abolish. Sadder for the country people was the loss of their twelve days' holiday. Yet they continued to keep Plough Monday, even though it no longer marked the resumption of work, and to collect "Light Money", although they had forgotten the meaning of the name. Part of the money had anyway been spent on a feast at the day's end; and that was kept up.

> Good huswives whom God hath enriched enow
> forget not the feasts that belong to the plough.
> The meaning is onely to joy and be glad
> for comfort with labour should sometimes be had.†

It should. But the counsel was destined to be forgotten. The age of the machine lay ahead, and a more desolate conception of man's traffic with the earth.

Plough Monday might be held to have lost its *raison d'être* altogether. Not only did it cease long ago to be the first working day after Christmas, but most of the ploughing

---

* Iolo A. Williams, *English Folk-Song and Dance*, 1935.
† Thomas Tusser, *Five Hundred Points of Good Husbandry*, 1580.

is now done in the Autumn. The objection is not as weighty as it seems, for the practice cannot be described as new. In the margins of a mediæval Book of Hours one may see the ploughman at work in September, the sower in the following month. Spring ploughing continues; and plough matches are often held on this day. In fact the festival has begun to show new signs of life. We might regard it as the New Year's Day of agriculture.

In the high street of a West Country town in the Winter before the war, a group of young men might be found on this morning in traditional costume, dancing the Sword Dance for a puzzled audience of shopping-women. We may wonder if such "instances of agility" (to employ a phrase of Brand's) however well managed—and this was—could ever again be anything but 'quaint' to the countryman: a damning epithet. In any case local enthusiasm hardly amounts to a revival. Whether we can apply that word to the new interest taken by the Church in the agricultural festivals remains to be seen. There are four of them: Plough Sunday, Rogation-tide, Lammas and Harvest Thanksgiving. Together they embrace the complete cycle of husbandry: ploughing and sowing, the young corn, the first fruits, the ingathering. The festivals are old, but in the last century the first three evoked no response at all from the Church of England. Now the Council for the Church and Countryside, instituted in 1943, attempts to revive them. Salisbury and Chichester appear to have taken the lead, and the Bishop of Salisbury has written a temporary service for each of the four occasions.* During the Plough Sunday service a plough is once again brought to the chancel entrance in the mediæval

* Published by the S.P.C.K. in a pamphlet entitled *The Church and the Land*. The Council for the Church and Countryside are now drafting four permanent services, with the help of certain eminent writers, and these will be published in a year or two, after trial and revision.

manner, farmers and ploughmen stand about it, and the priest or bishop invokes a blessing on their work. Thus it was done at Sherborne Abbey in 1943 and at Chichester Cathedral in 1946, the Lord Lieutenant and the Mayor attending, and a representative from the Ministry of Agriculture. And thus it has been done in many small churches without the help of such dignified persons. It might be supposed that the modern labourer would fail to respond, but that apparently is not the case. The difficulty that confronted one clergyman in the Salisbury diocese during the war "was not to get enough ploughmen to stand by the plough, but to find enough room for those who wish to do so".

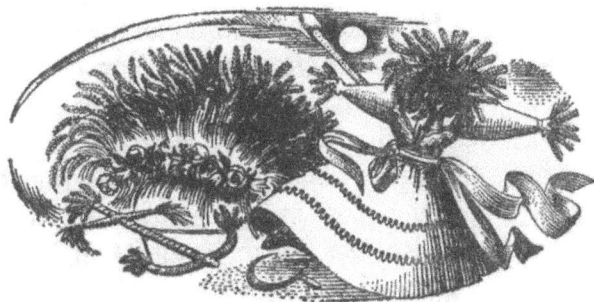

CANDLEMAS

FEBRUARY 2ND

Now—now, as low I stooped, thought I,
I will see what this snowdrop is;
So shall I put much argument by,
    And solve a lifetime's mysteries.
                    WALTER DE LA MARE—'*The Snowdrop*'

IN honour of the purification of the Virgin, and of the presentation in the Temple, and of Simeon, who exclaimed, "a light to lighten the Gentiles", the early Church instituted on February 2nd the Feast of Lights, blessed her candles, placed by the altar in sheaves, and filled her basilicas with candleshine. Then the faithful took up every one a wax candle—an object of wonder outside a church—and walked through the town in procession. That was the answer to the torches men were still waving in the streets of Rome after centuries of Christianity, for the Lupercalia died hard. Outside shut doors the diabolic shindy continued, but within all was vibration and amazement of light. "I beseech thee that thou wouldst bless this thy creature of wax. . ." "I bless thee, O thou waxen creature, in the name of our Lord. . ." "Thus," said the Pope, "what was done before to the honour of Ceres, is now done to the honour of the Virgin."* The torches vanished. The candles prevailed.

They prevailed, too, in Saxon England, where Ælfric the homilist wrote of the custom in 1050. It was well kept up through the Middle Ages, but in the reign of Edward VI was held to have become an idolatry, and perhaps it had;

* Quoted by William Hone, *The Every-Day Book*, Vol. I, Col. 202.

though why one form of matter is less profane than another, why stone may be blessed but wax may not, why a church may be consecrated, but not the candles that will brighten the church, are difficult questions. So the Church of England ceased to *bless* her candles, though not to light them. "On Candlemas Daye," ran an order in the reign of Henry VIII, "it shall be declared that the bearynge of candels is done to the memorie of Christe, the spirituall lyghte, whom Simeon dyd prophecye, as it is redde in the churche that daye." A century later Dr. Donne was heard defending in St. Paul's this "admitting of candles into the church, because He Who was the Light of the Worlde was on this day of Lighte brought into the Temple of the Lord". But the Puritans did not agree. In 1628 one of them, a pre-bendary of Durham, observed with disrelish the whimsical behaviour of the bishop's chaplain, John Cosin, later a celebrated bishop himself, and felt moved to complain about it in writing. "On Candlemas Day last past, Mr. Cozens, in renuing that popish ceremonie of burning candles in the honour of Our Ladye, busied himself from two of the clocke in the afternoon till foure, in climbing long ladders to stick up wax candles in the said Cathedral Church. The number of all the Candles burnt that evening was two hundred and twenty, besides sixteen torches: sixty of those burning tapers and torches standing upon, and near, the High Altar (as he calls it), where no man came nigh."* During the Commonwealth they hoped to put out the feast of lights for ever in England. But they were only successful to a point. A writer to the *Gentleman's Magazine* in 1790 noticed at Ripon that "the collegiate church was one continued blaze of light all the afternoon, from an immense number of candles". To-day, in all Roman Catholic churches,

* See John A. Bouquet, *Christmas to Candlemas*, 1931, p. 57.

and in some Anglican ones, the feast of lights is remembered, and there is much blessing and processing with tapers.

"With some, Christmas ends with the Twelve Days, but with the Generality of the Vulgar, not till Candlemas."* Nowhere is that any longer true: Christmas appears to be quite remote from Candlemas. The day is little more than a milestone in earliest Spring. Behind lie the gaieties of mid-winter; ahead, bleak Lent with a warm skyline.—

> Candlemas come and gone,
> The snow lies on a hot stone.

Walter de la Mare's murmured question, overheard at the beginning of this chapter, had been answered many centuries before it was put, perhaps not less well than he answered it himself in the poem, though differently. Snowdrops are 'Mary's Tapers'—'Candlemas Bells.' They are the day's particular flower, a symbol of purity: like a signal too, a lifted finger; flowing in over the rubbish of the wood's bottom, the first high C of Spring.

Some say they came to us from the Crimea in the seventeenth century, but that would appear to be only the larger kind, *Galanthus plicatus*. According to one authority, J. T. B. Syme, the author of *English Botany*, the common snowdrop, *Galanthus nivalis*, may have been native at the foot of the Herefordshire Beacon, and at Wrexham in Wales. This notion appears to be supported by an old custom peculiar to that part of the island: a bowl of snow-drops on Candlemas Day was held to give a house "the white purification". If native, the flower was not widely known. Shakespeare never refers to it. In 1664 John Evelyn wrote of "snow flowers or drops", and that is about the earliest reference we have.

* Henry Bourne, *Antiquitates Vulgares*, 1725.

CANDLEMAS. FEBRUARY 2ND.

At Candlemas in the South of England a wax candle was
lit at nightfall. The children stayed up, and punch was
made, and bedtime was when the flame burnt itself out.
To-day, for a children's party, snowdrops are put in bowls
and a number of white candles may be wound with ribbon
in the manner of the Christmas candles already described.*
But the effect will be different; for now the colour is blue
or silver, and when they are first lit the twilight of a
February evening has hardly begun to fall.

ST. VALENTINE'S DAY
FEBRUARY 14TH

*But, say they, it induceth loove. So say I also, but
what loove?*

PHILIP STUBBES—*Anatomie of Abuses*, 1583

NOTHING, one is prompted to say, could be more
innocently playful than a Valentine, yet its origin is a little
indelicate. Like the candles of Candlemas, recently gone by,
it comes to us by direct descent from the Lupercalia of pagan
Rome, that long February festival whose obstinate refusal
to die so exercised the ingenuity of the early Fathers. It
was about the middle of the month that the names of
willing young ladies were put in a box and well shaken up,
so that each young blood could draw out one at random;
the girl thus won to remain his companion while the gaieties
lasted. After a few centuries of denunciation the Church
perceived that she must change her tactics. Bad customs,
rooted in the atavistic twilight, could be altered, made
harmless, and even in the end helpful to her, but they could
not be abolished by edict. Accordingly, just as she instituted
Candlemas, to outshine the torches with her long pro-
cessions of candlelight, so did she set herself to correct this
even more unsavoury feature of the Lupercalian orgy.
Evidently, a lottery there must be. Then let dead saints
replace the living courtesans in the box. They did. The
people were invited to draw the name of a saint at random,
to whom prayers would be offered. And obscure St.

Valentine, whose feast it was, lent to the day—or else acquired from it—his reputation for unusual warmth of heart.

Yet, as it turned out, there was more willingness to exchange torches for candles than to accept the other substitute. The peculiar privileges of the season extended right across Europe to our own rude ancestors, and they too were regrettably conservative. Nature herself seemed to bolster their conservatism.—Did not the very birds choose their mates on St. Valentine's Day? For all that, the Church had her way in the end, as she is apt to do. Though centuries passed and still the lottery for girls continued, now under the respectable patronage of a saint, the full implications were presently forgotten, and what began as a debauch evolved into a game. "It is a ceremony, never omitted among the Vulgar," wrote Bourne in 1725, "to draw lots which they term Valentines. The names of a select number of one sex are by an equal number of the other put into some vessel; and after that, everyone draws a name, which for the present is called their Valentine, and is also look'd upon as a good omen of their being man and wife afterwards."

There had been nothing ominous about the original custom, in that sense. But times had changed. There was now, too, another way of acquiring a Valentine, and here both chance and choice were involved. According to this tradition, it was the first man seen by a woman that morning, outside her household, who became her Valentine willy-nilly, and he hers, and neither then could look for another. This thought was amusing Pepys on February 14th, 1661, when he left home early to make sure of his Valentine. "Up early and to Sir W. Batten's, but could not go in till I asked whether they that opened the door was a man or a woman. But Mingo (the manservant) in a feigned voice, answered a woman, which with his tone made me laugh; so up I went, and took Mrs. Martha for my Valentine (which I do only for complacency), and then Sir W. Batten he go in the same manner to my wife, and so we were very merry."

Next year his wife was more seriously exercised by the thought. "This morning comes in W. Bowyer, who was my wife's Valentine, she having (at which I made good sport with myself) held her hands all the morning that she might not see the paynters that were at work gilding my chimney-piece." It was well for a woman to save herself for a good Valentine, since a handsome present would follow. Sir William Batten, of the previous year, subsequently sent Mrs. Pepys "half a dozen pairs of gloves and a pair of silk stockings and garters". These gifts, of a vaguely symbolic sort, were usual—though a very rich man would give jewellery. "The Duke of York, being Mrs. Stewart's Valentine, did give her a jewel of about £800." Pepys knew the older method as well; for on one occasion he recorded that his "Cousin Turner drawd him", and that it would cost him about 28 shillings in presents; and another year "Mrs. The. showed me my name upon her breast, which will cost me 20 shillings". This way of extracting suitable tribute from the male was no doubt a sophisticated version of the country game.

True love had never cared for such games. True love had always employed the saint on a definite mission. As long ago as 1479 a girl was writing a letter "Unto my ryght wele-beloved Valuntyne, John Paston".* Letters of the kind were written for the next three hundred years; and then at last— but no, not at last, for to-day the amorous have found still another vehicle for their passion—there appeared in the February letter-box what we now call "the Victorian Valentine".

* There are many references to St. Valentine in the Paston Letters.

The name is altogether misleading. The "Valentine", understood to mean the creature of paper rather than the creature of flesh and blood by whom it would be opened, *agitato*, was not an invention of the Victorians. They inherited it from the Georgians; just as we inherit the Christmas tree from *them*. Indeed, the present writer believes that no date of origin can be offered, however tentatively—that the origins of the custom go back to the England of the Stuarts, if not to the England of *The Paston Letters*. Once more we will call on Pepys to give evidence, and underline a part of his statement. "This morning," he records in 1667, "came up to my wife's bedside little Will Mercer to be her Valentine, and brought *her name written upon blue paper in gold letters*, done by himself very prettily, and we both very well pleased with it." If this morsel of home-made calligraphy appears to be rather remote from the fully developed article by the firm of Marcus Ward two centuries later, we must remember that the earliest Valentines we possess are *all* home-made. They belong to the second half of the eighteenth century, and the oldest, in the Hull Museum, has been dated 1750. Another, of 1760—and a very fine example—is in the form of a song: poem, tune and pictured headpiece—

> "Charming Chloe, look with pity
> On your love-sick swain.   ."*

So good a Valentine deserved to be put aside, when others, simpler and cruder, were smiled at, only to be consigned to the flames. Often they were amateurish enough; a sketch of hearts and cupids, a touch of colour, a handful of couplets written all round the page, North, East, South and West.

---

* Photograph in Victoria and Albert Museum collection.

Few were kept, for few at the time were thought to be worth the keeping. How many were sent is difficult to estimate. The custom appears to have spread in the 1780's and '90's, and it was clearly in harmony with the age of sentiment. Yet the home-made "Valentine letter" could never have become the rage; it would always have been held within bounds for an obvious reason: not everyone had the skill to compose it. The saint was waiting for the nineteenth century craftsman.

The nineteenth century craftsman was not slow to respond. Like the Christmas card, but a good half century earlier, the commercial Valentine began as a form of stationery. Embossing of notepaper was fashionable under the Regency, and many of these early examples are finely embossed. In the most charming, from the workshop of Dobbs, a group in the centre is surrounded by little mottoes, mostly written in French, the language of gallantry. Sometimes they were delivered by hand, but far more often by the postman. Envelopes were then unknown—they were hardly in use before 1840—and Valentines were folded like the letters of the period, and put through the post; often we can date them precisely from the postmark they carry on the back. Indeed, they *were* letters of a kind; only now the sender was not put to the test of composition: he could buy one to his liking ready-made, in a shop. Frequently he preferred not to do so; for if he fancied himself with pencil and paint brush, or at turning a neat couplet, no bought verbosity, no standardised love-knots would content him. It is well to realise that the made-up Valentine was in truth a confession of failure, like the made-up tie. Both are a substitute for the fruit and reward of labour—for a contrivance a little lame in the knot, perhaps, and a bit lopsided, but at any rate the composer's own, the one veritable transitory flower of personal inspiration. Aware that, for all their embossing and gilding, their lacing and trimming, they would never achieve the "personal touch", the stationers modestly made allowances for it. *Some* Valentines they produced *half-finished*, and presented the purchaser with a little parcel of oddments to conclude the design in his own manner; which he did, much less effectively, of course, than the firm. The tradition of the home-made Valentine did not die at once. The writer has seen a mid-Victorian box containing a set of tools, gums and raw materials required in the manufacture of these ephemeræ. However, the later the year, the richer the style, and the wider the gap between amateur and professional. In the end it was hardly possible to compete with a designer employing a hundred skilful operatives, and the home-made Valentine vanished.

But we have advanced too quickly, and must return to Regency London. St. Valentine certainly depended on the Post Office for the efficiency of his latest weapon, now fully developed. In days when the post was slow and expensive, he could never have used it. Now a twopenny letter in London would claim—and thus by extending the sense of the word, would itself become—a "Valentine". The possibility offered immediate scope for wit and sentiment, and above all secrecy: for the entwining of initials, for the authorship ardently hinted, for the rhymed anonymous heartbreak— and of course for the heartless leg-pull. In 1825 the London Post Office handled two hundred thousand more letters on St. Valentine's Day than on any other, and each year the number increased. We read already in Elia of the "bestuck and bleeding heart" and of "the finest gilt paper" glittering with rhymes and mottoes and devices, Leander in the choppy water, Thisbe piled on Pyramus, and other allegorical pale incidents.　　　And all, still, in the April of the tender missive.

Full summer arrived with the Queen, the envelope, and the new techniques. To these benefits one would add the Universal Penny Post, introduced in 1840, if that did not seem to have had no effect on the custom. There were probably few who dispatched more than two or three Valentines, so that a penny more or less on the postage made little difference. Neither did the halfpenny post of 1870 affect the numbers. They continued to rise at a normal rate, until in 1880 a million and a half were sent off.* Three or four hundred additional workers had to be employed on February 13th. They stood ankle-deep in the letters, which came through the slit in a continuous shower, till the baskets overflowed on the floor. And then there were Valentine parcels and Valentine hampers; and sometimes a very large hamper would be brought to a door, out of which there would leap a very small boy, dressed up like a Cupid.

To embossing the 1820's had added lithographing. To both the 1840's were now adding the use of lace, hand-painted satin, and a variety of ornaments applied to the surface of the paper, so that the Valentine began, as it were, to rise above itself. Secure in a sumptuous envelope, and later in a trim cardboard box, it ventured on a third dimension. Then, beneath the sun of humid sentiment that nourished the Keepsake and the Album, the Valentine broke into a pimply froth of lace; its leaves became plural, studded with birds, baskets, ribbons and Cupids—Cupid always the Saint's attendant, as the robin was Father Christmas's—

---

* In 1825, 200,000. In 1855, 800,000. A curious decline in the early 1860's. Then a steady increase from 1865 to 1,634,000 in 1882. Figures supplied by the G.P.O. Librarian. Other information in this paragraph from *The Post Office Magazine* for February, 1937.

its petals turned pink and gold, opening into trellis-work doors, one beneath another, to reveal at last the trembling delicacy of a rhyme. And it acquired perfume. Even so did this rutilant, anaglyptic and nostalgic filament of sensibility draw a veil, if only of forget-me-nots, over its deplorable ancestry. How long a journey from the Lupercalian ballot-box!

But already the art was decaying, as all arts decay when they become too profitable. A huge market necessitates mass production; and popular taste fell off disastrously in the second half of the reign. The extremely elaborate Valentines of the 1860's and 70's, covered with bits of real grass and moss, real feathers, and other imported 'scraps', are certainly not without charm, but they lack the delicacy that Dobbs and others gave to their work in the years before the Great Exhibition. It was during this period that the Valentine and the Christmas card (of one sort) drew near in resemblance, being made by the same craftsmen; until, round about 1885, they diverged again on their different roads to vulgarity.

One of those who went in for a good deal of ebullience and fluff was Eugene Rimmel, a celebrated *parfumeur* in the Strand, and apparently a latecomer to the Valentine trade. Most of his materials came from George Meek, the fancy stationer of Fleet Street, in whose workshop one would have discovered gilding and silvering, cutting out of patterns, embossing, lacing, perforating, folding and trimming, all being done at the same moment; while elsewhere the lithographer, the draftsman, the wood engraver, the cardboard-maker, the artificial florist, the worker in silk, in feathers, in glass, in filigree and in lacquer, were all contributing to the pleasure and profit of the Happy Family over which Eugene Rimmel presided. So he did not exactly construct his Valentines; they were only, we learn, "composed, put

together and made delicious with fragrance by Mr. Rimmel."
But that was an industry in itself. From eighty to a hundred
women were constantly at work according to the time of
year, and Rimmel hovered around them with a watchful eye,
thinking up new ideas with "the unforeseen addition of
strange and quaint materials, whimsical surprises and
practical jests". He liked the larger, three-dimensional
Valentines too (he sold them for several guineas apiece): a
looking-glass lake with a swan: a sweet-box hidden in a
"satin couch", a musical box that chimed in a posy of flowers.
Rimmel sought his ingredients all over the world: in Genoa
and Budapest, in Peru, Bohemia and Japan. One year he
discovered a Brazilian convent where the nuns were making
artificial flowers out of the feathers of gorgeous tropical
birds. "It is Nature imitating Nature!" he cried.*

Alongside the tender Valentine there had grown to a sort
of wry-faced maturity the comic. This owed nothing to the
ornamental stationer, but a great deal to the maker of the
chapbook and street ballad—an ancient fraternity. It is true
that popular Valentines, printed on paper and brightly
coloured, were not always humorous, but they were
frequently so. Sometimes the humour was contrived by a
simple mechanism. Beneath a picture of a girl in a crinoline
there is a rhyme warning the recipient not to go out in a
high wind. When a ribbon is pulled at the top of the card
the skirt rises coyly to her ankles, revealing the lace-edged
extremity of a pair of drawers. Much more often the joke
was too unkind to be funny: tears rather than giggles seem
to have been the sender's intention. "As we grow older the
glass loses its charm."—A glass of wine lifts up to reveal
a scrawny old woman glooming at herself in the looking-

* See *The Illustrated London News*, February 14th, 1874, for a detailed
article on the work of Rimmel, Meek, and Marcus Ward.

glass. Cruel, too, in their sprightly way, would be the
following words if torn from a deceptively ingratiating
envelope, and scanned by a lumpish young lady:

> Were you more like fair Hebe, or sweet Venus,
> I would perform with you the Polka caper,
> And there should really be a dance between us
> Too joyous to be well expressed on paper.
> But as you have no beauty to inspire me
> I must decline with you all Polka Dancing,
> And seek some lovelier Valentine to fire me,
> And then the Polka will be quite entrancing!

By the time these words were written, even the true
Valentines—the ardent, the tender, or the merely polite—
were falling from grace. And still they contrive to appear
in the stationer's window to-day, stripped of all but a weary
mechanical sentiment. Yet although in our age no Valentine,
one half as elaborate as the best from Marcus Ward, could
be sold in the shops to any but the rich, or the desperately
enamoured—might not artist and poet combine to evolve,
with profit, a few shillingsworth of grace in contemporary
terms? They might: if the recent 'revival' of the Valentine,
along with other forms of Victoriana, is any indication. Old
Valentines have been sought in bureaux, have been placed
in antique shop windows, have been put through the post,
and treasured.

But a 'revival' in inverted commas is not a revival with
roots in the soil of contemporary living. Even as at
Christmas, where the Cards are in need of a new inspiration,
opportunity awaits the imaginative artist, or printer, or
manufacturer, and the market, we know, is not deserted.
For already, and for the second time, the Post Office has
found the right stimulant for the saint. In 1935 it invited

the writer's brother, Rex Whistler, to provide the first 'St. Valentine's Telegram'. Copies of the gay-coloured form he designed, larger than usual and printed on better paper, were issued to every office of delivery, in advance. By the end of that day 49,000 had been despatched to the fair in golden envelopes. The ordinary Greetings Telegram, intended for use on any day in the year, had been introduced in 1935. By this time 15,000 of these were sent every week, or roughly 2,100 on any one day. Allowing that some of those handed in on February 14th were 'ordinary greetings', this would seem to indicate that nearly 47,000 Valentines were claimed by the new method—not many, indeed, when compared with Victorian practice, yet a remarkable proof that the festival is not dead; especially if we bear in mind the many thousands of Valentines bought in the shops each year, since the custom was revived in 1929.*

A Valentine sent on his form is reproduced on the opposite page, though, not, alas in glittering colour, and not quite as it reached the recipient, in the handwriting of the local postmistress; for *that* copy is not available. Every year a fresh artist provided the design, and the success of the venture was maintained, until the war brought it to a temporary standstill.

Now there is one thing more we would ask of those enterprising authorities before they hand back to St. Valentine, our benevolent Pandarus, the latest, if not the last, of all his many devices. The verse reproduced in the illustration did in fact arrive at its destination in good shape. Not so every Valentine verse. Some cf them came out very lamely in the form of prose. It seems that what the telegraph offices require is a little instruction in prosody. What better than a directive from the Postmaster General himself?

* Figures supplied by the G.P.O.

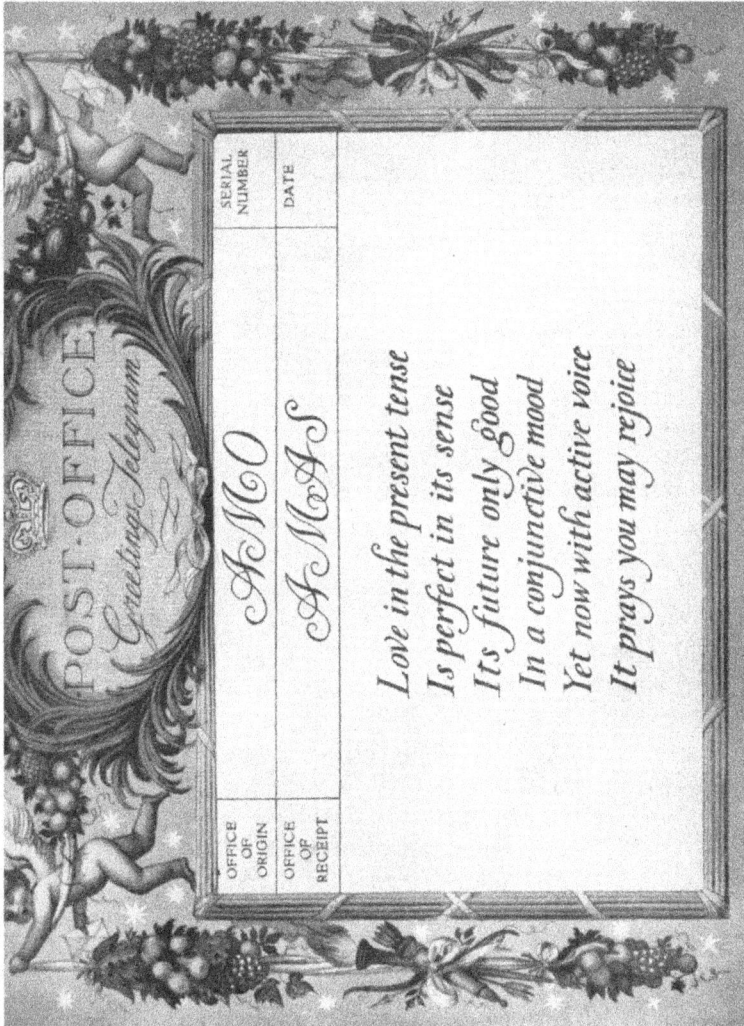

POST·OFFICE

Greetings Telegram

| OFFICE OF ORIGIN | ANO | SERIAL NUMBER |
| OFFICE OF RECEIPT | ANAS | DATE |

Love in the present tense
Is perfect in its sense
Its future only good
In a conjunctive mood
Yet now with active voice
It prays you may rejoice

ST. VALENTINE'S TELEGRAM FORM DESIGNED BY REX WHISTLER   [Reprinted by courtesy of the G.P.O.]

Showing a verse sent on February 14th. The form was in bright colours. See p. 100.

SHROVE TUESDAY

THE EVE OF LENT*

Fritter-fild, as well as heart can wish.

PASQUIL—*Palinodia*, 1634

THE Tuesday that follows the first eyelash of a new moon in February is the last of the three days of Shrovetide: preceded by Quinquagesima Sunday and Shrove Monday. The name is connected with the verb to shrive, for on this day, the Eve of Ash Wednesday, the penitent received absolution and prepared himself for the rigours of Lent. Those who were about to keep Lent seriously would first keep Shrovetide with proportionate gaiety, for the forty days lasted until Easter Eve, and during that time there would be no indulgence. If there was any forbidden food in the larder it had to be finished, and the good housewife made sure that there was. Shrove Monday was also Collop Monday, the day on which eggs and collops of meat appeared on the table, and that was farewell to flesh and fowl. Shrove Tuesday was Pancake Tuesday, for with the stroke of midnight butter and fat would be exiled. Yet the festival pancake is derived, like so many customs of the faithful, from a heathen observance—similar to the Roman Fornacalia—and so too were the cock-fighting and street football, the gaming and clowning once proper to Shrovetide and even in the present century not wholly suppressed. Shrove

* The moon determines the date of Easter, and Easter determines the dates of the movable festivals described in this book. A table, showing the dates of those festivals every year until the year 1975, will be found in Appendix A.

[101]

Tuesday had been always a whole holiday for the apprentices. Brand warned them, as long ago as 1776, that they ought "with that watchful Jealousy of their antient Rights and Liberties which becomes the young Englishman, to guard against every Infringement of its Ceremonies, and transmit them entire and unadulterated to Posterity"; but this they neglected to do. Brand guessed that in less than a century they would lose their pancakes. There he was wrong. These continue to make in the frying pan what Taylor, the water-poet, described as "a confused dismall hissing"; and the Westminster boys continue to scramble, and the cameras to click while they do it. Newspapers do not always kill customs, by making them quaint. In the last resort the publicity they give may be a means of keeping them alive.

MOTHERING SUNDAY

THE FOURTH SUNDAY IN LENT*

That thy days may be long upon the land.

Exodus XX: 12

IN matriarchal America there is now, fittingly enough, a day for honouring the American mother. It falls on the second Sunday in May, and is known as Mother's Day. The celebration is rather interesting. It is the best modern example, in the Anglo-Saxon world, of a newly invented custom achieving immense popularity. This is the story of Mother's Day.

On May 9th, 1906, a certain Miss Anna Jarvis of Philadelphia lost her mother. Next year she invited a friend to keep the anniversary with her, and explained the plan she had formed. It was nothing less than to induce the entire American people to honour their mothers on a particular day. It must have seemed to that friend a for-midable task, but Miss Jarvis had fire and fervour within her; she certainly had 'drive'. She talked, she wrote letters, she buttonholed public men; and she succeeded—even more quickly than she had dared to hope. The very next year, on the second anniversary of her loss, Philadelphia publicly observed the day. Then the tempo of her efforts increased. Interviews were implored, thousands of letters were written, matricultural cells were formed; till State after State succumbed to that importunate tenderness. In Pennsylvania a State holiday—in Texas a day for pardoning

* See Appendix A.

prisoners—in all churches a service—in all schools an empty classroom on Friday—clearly the maternal festival called for a node of activity (she was that herself), with a ramification of branch-offices, a propaganda wide as the continent, and a white carnation for badge. "Through some distinct act of kindness, visit, letter, gift or tribute, to show remembrance of the mother to whom your affection is due": that was to be the slogan. Her efforts were crowned when on May 10th, 1913, the Senate and the House of Representatives officially dedicated the day "to the memory of the best mother in the world, *your* mother".* In the Victorian Englishman's home the Christmas tree could not have been planted by anyone humbler than a Prince. In "the century of the common man", and in the nation that boasts of belonging to it, how appropriate that a private citizen should originate Mother's Day!

Among the countless American soldiers who helped to garrison England for two or three years there were some who came to regard their English hostess in the light of a foster-mother. These well-disposed young men observed our apparent lack of a similar custom and determined to remedy it as well as they could, within the limits of war-time frugality. They entertained her, they showed their affection in that distinct act of kindness, visit, letter, gift or tribute. Reports appeared in the newspapers, and some suggested that we ought, after all, to adopt the custom ourselves, though earlier attempts to make us do so had failed. Certainly the Christmas tree has demonstrated that a foreign custom will take root if it receives a good deal of publicity. The American soldiers of 1943 might improve our habits in the same way that the Germans at Manchester, and the Prince Consort at Windsor, improved them a century earlier.

* *Encyclopedia Americana.*

They do not seem to have done so. Perhaps they departed too soon, for this purpose; or perhaps there were too few of them who cared to keep Mother's Day in a foreign land. Or again it may be that an English family is still too patriarchal in structure. As well, there is this to be said: it was not *our* public men that Miss Jarvis buttonholed; her example excites our wonder more than it fires our enthusiasm. Overriding all other considerations, if we do decide to pay tribute to a few million more of the best mothers in the world, a better occasion could be found—a better occasion already exists—than the second Sunday in May. For centuries we have possessed a 'Mother's Day', but we called it Mothering Sunday. There are English children taught to remember it still.

At the Roman Hilaria, and in the North under other names, honour had been done to the Mother of the Gods. But names did not mean very much in that early England. The baptised pagan, still a pagan at heart, was content to bring his gifts to another building, or to the same building furnished with different symbols, and to lay them at the altar of Mother Church. He honoured the idea of mother-hood, and his descendants in Protestant England, especially in the western counties, continued to honour that idea in their mother's house. On that Sunday, the fourth in Lent, they would visit her with a trinket, or a bunch of early flowers, or a cake of that special kind which Herrick mentioned in a poem:

> I'le to thee a Simnell bring,
> 'Gainst thou go'st a mothering.
> So that, when she blesseth thee,
> Half that blessing thou'lt give me.

Gift and blessing were meant to symbolise the renewal of

home life or the unity of the family, continuing still, though physically divided by marriage. 'Simnel' appears to be derived from '*simila*', the Latin word for the finest wheat flour. There are three kinds of Simnel cake, each named after a town. The Shrewsbury kind has a thick crust; the Devizes kind is in the shape of a star, crustless; the Bury kind is flattish, but thicker in the centre, compounded of spices, currants and candied peel, and generally round in shape or elongated. Before the war these cakes were sold in large quantities about the middle of Lent, and a good many of them found their way to the Dominions and the United States of America. Cakes of the Shrewsbury type were on sale in London and Watford in 1934, garnished with little fruits, artificial flowers, eggs and nests. In the following year they were specially advertised for Mothering Sunday.*

In the East End of London and in a number of country parishes, a special service for children is held on this day. The children take bunches of violets to the altar for a blessing, and return to their pews to offer them to their mothers.

* A. R. Wright and T. E. Lones, *British Calendar Customs: England*, 1936–8, Vol. I.

ALL FOOLS' DAY

APRIL 1ST

April is the cruellest month.
T. S. ELIOT—*The Waste Land*

"A TIME of festive celebration, a festal day; also occasionally, a merry-making": such is the definition of a festival given by the Dictionary. On the strength of that occasional meaning the April Fool is thought to deserve a humble place in this book. He is the subject of a merry-making, if not a participator in it—a merry-making trivial enough, yet one of great interest. For he is the chief surviving example of ancient Folly—a word that implied the *function* of foolishness, rather than a state. Other examples are not wanting: the Fool in the Sword Dance and the Revesby Play, and the Fool who capers around the Morris Dancers. These figures of rustic fun, no longer funny, are descended from a character whose part in the ritual must have seemed to himself fairly serious.* Behind the Fool we glimpse the Victim. On a certain day in Spring, it would seem, that part would be allotted at random; and the day was the octave of the old New Year on March 25th. How seriously the victim played his part, or, when seriously, how long ago, we cannot be sure. Nothing but the randomness of a prank remains. The April Fool is Everyman still, or at least he may still be any man.

* See Sir James Frazer, *The Golden Bough*, Part III, Chap. VIII, Sec. 3.

Between midnight and noon on April 1st everyone is liable to be made a fool of; for it is the morning of the practical joke. But it is not enough to discomfort the victim: he must be induced to take action himself, sent on a 'fool's errand', or anyway beguiled into some kind of credulous response; such is the character of April malice. There were formerly a number of stock deceptions for the use and abuse of children, each concluded, when successful, with the cry of "April Fool!" A child would be sent to the dairy for a pint of dove's milk, or to the bookseller for *The Life of Eve's Mother*, or to the ironmonger for a pennyworth of strap oil (delivered on the rump); but this trickery is rather *vieux jeu*. Practical jokes on a bigger scale have often been played, especially by undergraduates. Chambers records that in 1860 a vast number of persons received an invitation to the Tower of London of a very official appearance: "Admit the Bearer and Friend to view the Annual Ceremony of Washing the White Lions." Precisely the same trick had been played in 1698.* On the second occasion, many were simple enough to attend, in spite of the wording. To-day, an altered voice on the telephone has provided the malicious with a weapon to which the right answer has not yet been found.

Then, on the stroke of noon, it is finished. If anyone attempts devilry thereafter, even while the clock is still striking, it recoils on his head. A child would then race through the sing-song formula: "April-Fool-Day's-past-and-gone-you're-the-fool-and-I-am-none!" Why it should be so remains a mystery; but the law is rigid. Old curiosity could not explain it, though it found ingenious explanations of the custom itself. The original Fool, some believed, was hopeful Noah, who released a dove on the first day of the month

* Drake's *News-Letter*. It was probably a traditional joke in London.

when the whole surface of the world was covered with water: to commemorate his credulity fools have been made ever since at the abating of Winter.   Others remembered Proserpine, picking wild daffodils in a gorge when Pluto pounced: her scream, they said, echoed in the rocks, and Ceres went running in the wrong direction.   This notion may be nearer the truth.   Proserpine was an emblem of the buried seed, consigned to the underworld in winter, given back in the ecstasy of vernal green.   All the rites of Spring that we understand can be traced to that process of archaic apprehension and wonder, or to the renewal of courage in the sun.   This ritual—wide as the ancient world, and wider still, for India has its April Fools—may be no exception.   We know too little.   What is shadowed in all this foolery? What happened at the prick of noon, that moment when the sun stood upright?

PALM SUNDAY

THE SUNDAY BEFORE EASTER*

The house-roofs seemed to heave and sway.
ROBERT BROWNING—*The Patriot*

ON this Sunday, when boughs were bare and winds sharp in our dilatory Spring, it was the custom to go out into the woods and water-meadows, and cut, and bring into the house long wands of the willow or sallow, thick-studded with velvety buds, grey, pale-yellow or delicately pink, softer to touch than the bumble-bees they resembled. About a century ago, when the woods and fields round London were still only a moderate walk from the centre— though year by year the gas lamps pushed them further away—the men and boys went 'palming' in good numbers. Presently they could be seen returning, slips of willow in their hats, buds of willow in their buttonholes, and even between their lips, and with their hands full of the branches. But these were townsmen: in the maze of new brickwork no accurate knowledge of flora survived. To them the tree that they robbed was simply the palm, the authentic palm. And why did they rob it? Many could hardly have told us. They had always done it; and the expedition in an April dawn was enjoyable. If any were better informed, they certainly imagined those very same boughs thrown down on the road to Jerusalem.

"And a very great multitude spread their garments in the

* See Appendix A.

way: others cut down branches from the trees, and strawed them in the way." In the Roman world, palm branches had always been strewn in the path of a hero. But here in the North, where the Mediterranean palm is unknown, we chose the willow to replace it because no other tree is so well advanced at this time of year. Brought into a warm room and stood in water, it continues to burgeon throughout Holy Week.

In the centuries before the Western Church was divided, we in England made much of this Sunday, when we brought our palms to the altar to be blessed. "I conjure thee, thou creature of flowers and branches. . ." We circled the church by opposite routes, one file with a cross wrapped up, representing the world before Christ; one file with a glittering jewelled cross, "pricked full of palms." No sooner had they met than "the bumbled cross vanished away", and then there was singing and waving of boughs, and the children throwing down flowers and cakes from the battlements.* So we walked in procession, "with the Blessed Sacrament reverently carried, as if it were Christ upon the Ass, with strawing of Bushes and Flowers, bearing of Palms, spreading and hanging of the richest Clothes, the Quire and Quiristers singing, the Children and the People. And all done," we thought, "in a very godly Ceremony, to the Honour of Christ, and the Memory of His Triumph upon this Day." But later we thought differently, and denounced the people we had been as if we were strangers to them, and so indeed we had become. "Your Palm-Sunday Procession was horrible Idolatry," we now declared, "you turn the Holy Mystery of Christ's riding to Jerusalem, to a May-game and Pageant Play."†

* Thomas Brecon, *The Potation of Lent*, 1542.
† Henry Bourne, *Antiquitates Vulgares*, ed. Brand, 1777, p. 237.

A reasonable practice may become corrupt, and then the unmaskers of that corruption may fall into an opposite error. Opinions vary. Better to observe that in many houses the willow boughs are still to be seen on Palm Sunday, and in many churches little strips of the true palm, now sent from Spain, are looped and folded into the shape of a cross, blessed at the altar and there given away.

GOOD FRIDAY

*I know not how my Reader will be satisfied with this
learned Writer's explication.*
                    JOHN BRAND—*Observations on Popular Antiquities*

THE date of the first Good Friday will never be known, but
many scholars believe that the event took place on April 7th,
A.D. 30. If they are right the calendar is wrong, by three
years. When a man dies in the parish of Ayot St. Peter in
Hertfordshire they ring the "Nine Tailors"—or "Tellers"—
followed by a bell tolling his age in years, and on this day
the bell tolls thirty-three times. Good Friday is the com-
plement of Easter, the shadow offsetting the light. That
shadow has a symbol in the three hours' service, and in
Tenebræ, the night office of Holy Week, when the candles
on the hearse are put out one by one.

Popular customs have to be pleasant or amusing; we
should not expect to find many attached to a time of
mourning and penitence. A correspondent of *The Times*
in 1944* observed at Hammersmith on Maundy Thursday,
the Eve of Good Friday, little gardens on the pavement,
"each planted with twelve tiny shoots of privet and protected
with branches." These were surely "Gardens of Adonis", the
same that had once been made for the dying God of the
Spring, and afterwards for the dying Christ. Once they
were more elaborate, and rather like those that are still to
be seen in Sicily: a delicate sepulchre of shells and branches,
with a candle burning inside. But a single instance in all
London does not constitute a living tradition of Holy Week:

* *The Times*, April 13th, 1944.

only the Hot Cross Buns could be described as that—those buns flavoured with allspice, and marked with the sign of the Cross, which are supposed to be eaten at breakfast, hot from the oven. Chambers wondered in 1864 if the buns of his youth had not been far more delicious, but that may have been an illusion. In his childhood they had certainly been more popular; for the keeping of the day had been much revived about the turn of the century. The custom had given to the dawn of Good Friday in London a sound unlike the sound of all other days in the year. The rattle of wheels and the sing-song cries of the working week were silenced, the shops and the factories closed. As the Londoner dressed himself, he could hear in the street nothing but the crying of certain phrases, by old voices and young: "Hot Cross Buns: One-a-penny Buns: Two-a-penny Buns: One-a-penny, Two-a-penny, Hot Cross Buns!" Somebody beckoned from a door, and the vendor hurried towards her. One corner of a white cloth, then the corner of a flannel beneath it, was carefully lifted from the basket, and as quickly as possible put back. For most of the morning the cries continued; then they were hushed while the churches filled; only to begin again in the afternoon.

Even this, the most apparently Christian of minor customs, cannot be claimed as a Christian invention. Two petrified loaves, five inches in diameter, were discovered at Herculaneum, both marked with a cross, and Herculaneum was overwhelmed in A.D. 79. It is very unlikely that these were made for a Christian. The Greeks, too, marked their bread in this way. But that will not account for the same custom among the Anglo-Saxons. Wheaten cakes marked with a cross may have been eaten at the Spring Festival by all primitive peoples, before the Gospel suggested another meaning. They were certainly eaten wherever Diana was worshipped, and her festival occurred at this time. In Hertfordshire, where the Roman Ermine Street crosses the still more ancient Icknield Way, the ruins have been found of an altar raised to "Diana of the Crossways". Is it mere coincidence that the neighbourhood has been noted for its Hot Cross Buns?*

Under the "holy pictures" in their classical beauty there extends a set of earlier scenes, the colour crude and the drawing clumsy, savage in conception, yet obviously similar. Beneath the agony and joy of the dead and risen Christ can be traced in unmistakable outline the ferocious stance of the Spring God. In mediæval England, on a day before Easter, the choirs would move through the churches carrying a piece of turf like a coffin, and all the while loudly bewailing the death of "Alleluia".† But the resurrection of that uncouth being they had long since forgotten to welcome: the bright impasto of Easter covered it up. Aware of these correspondences, a few have supposed that the later Figure is no more than a repainting of the earlier—they have doubted the very existence of an "historical Jesus". But a different interpretation offers itself. The ancient pictures might be sketches of a truth already existing in eternity but not yet actual on the plane of time: ideas received in supernatural hearsay, and recorded in pictures no more accurate than Ptolemey's map of Britain. Here and there, where the outlines diverge, the original work shows clearly: a bit of garland, spread fingers, a lamenting profile.

* P. H. Ditchfield, *Old English Customs*, 1896.
† Sources given by T. D. Fosbroke, *British Monachism*, 1802.

EASTER*

And then to awake, and the farm, like a wanderer white
With the dew, come back, the cock on his shoulder; it was all
Shining, it was Adam and maiden,
The sky gathered again
And the sun grew round that very day.
So it must have been after the birth of the simple light
In the first, spinning place, the spellbound horses walking warm
Out of the whinnying green stable
On to the fields of praise.

DYLAN THOMAS—'*Fern Hill*'

"WHEN we reflect," says Sir James Frazer, "how often the Church has skilfully contrived to plant the seeds of the new faith on the old stock of paganism, we may surmise that the Easter celebration of the dead and risen Christ was grafted upon a similar celebration of the dead and risen Adonis. . . The type, created by Greek artists, of the sorrowful goddess with her dying lover in her arms, resembles and may have been the model of the Pietà of Christian art, the Virgin with the dead body of her divine Son in her lap."† The Venerable Bede appears to corroborate this. From him we learn that the name Easter, peculiar to the English tongue, is derived from Éastre, or as he calls her, Eostre, the Goddess of Spring. Her month of April, known to the Anglo-Saxons as Éastor-monath, became the *mensis paschalis* of Christian England, "when the old festival was observed with the gladness of a new solemnity."

---

* See Appendix A for the date of Easter each year, up to the year 1975.

† Sir James Frazer, *The Golden Bough*, Part IV, Bk. 1, Chap. X, 'The Gardens of Adonis.'

EASTER

How much the *manner* of a Christian celebration may reflect an earlier rite can be judged from an account of Good Friday and Easter, as they used to be kept by the Orthodox Church in Athens. "During the whole of Good Friday a waxen effigy of the dead Christ is exposed to view in the middle of the Greek churches and is covered with fervent kisses by the thronging crowd, while the whole church rings with melancholy, monotonous dirges. Late in the evening, when it has grown quite dark, this waxen image is carried by the priests into the street on a bier adorned with lemons, roses, jessamine, and other flowers, and there begins a grand procession of the multitude, who move in serried ranks, with slow and solemn step, through the whole town. Every man carries his taper and breaks out into doleful lamentation. At all the houses which the procession passes there are seated women with censers to fumigate the marching host. Thus the community solemnly buries its Christ as if he had just died. At last the waxen image is again deposited in the church, and the same lugubrious chants echo anew. These lamentations, accompanied by a strict fast, continue till midnight on Saturday. As the clock strikes twelve, the bishop appears and announces the glad tidings that 'Christ is risen', to which the crowd replies, 'He is risen indeed,' and at once the whole city bursts into an uproar of joy, which finds vent in shrieks and shouts, in the endless discharge of carronades and muskets, and the explosion of fire-works of every sort. In the very same hour people plunge from the extremity of the fast into the enjoyment of the Easter lamb and neat wine."*

The Rites of Spring in the North were not so graciously kept as among the highly civilised peoples of the Mediter-

---

* C. Wachsmuth, *Das alte Griechenland in neuem*, quoted by Frazer. (See note above.)

ranean. Éastor-monath was a clumsier tree for ingrafting
the new religion. We know the kind of observance that was
paid then from the eggs and flowers of Easter, the candles
and new garments, and from certain curious frivolities kept
up in the last century. But the 'pace-egging' plays and the
ball games of Easter, the 'lifting' of women by men one
day, and of men by women the next, deserve only the
barest of mentions for they now belong to the lunar world
of the antiquarian, where nothing can alter. Certainly the
foreign monks who settled in England after the Conquest,
and the foreign priests who took up office here, enriched
the habits of the people, but Easter was already a great
occasion for the conquered Saxons. They acted the Resurrection in church, with a sepulchre beside the altar, and the
women arriving to find it bare. Presently they began to
make Easter carols, and towards the end of the Middle Ages
the Paschal dramas of England were no less elaborate than
those of the mainland. There was no secular stage in the
modern sense, and the people attended the pageants by
thousands, more for amusement than for edification, though
indeed they had hardly learnt to distinguish the two. That
was a cause of complaint among the reformers, earnestly
bent on recovering the simplicity of the Gospel. The poet
Chatterton possessed a manuscript of 1470, describing the
properties made that year for the Bristol play, and delivered
to the Vicar of St. Mary Redcliffe.—"A new Sepulchre, well
guilt with fine gold; an image of God Almighty rising out of
the same Sepulchre. Item, Heven, made of timber and
stained cloths. Item, Hell, made of timber and iron Work,
with Devils the number of thirteen. Item, four knights
armed, keeping the Sepulchre, with their weapons in their
hands. Item four pair of Angel's wings, for four Angels,
made of timber, and well-painted. Item, the Holy Ghost

coming out of Heven into the Sepulchre. Item, the Fadre, the crown and visage, well gilt with fine gold."*

February had had its candles, but Easter quite out-candled Candlemas. The reader may remember how Candlemas transformed Durham Cathedral into a lantern. At Easter, in the Middle Ages, a greater wonder was seen in that church, as in many others. The Paschal Candle rose, square in section, to within a man's length of the roof, where it was lit by "a fine convenience". But first, on Easter Eve, the building was in darkness; and then the new fire, emblem of the Resurrection, was kindled by flint and steel at the top of this waxen obelisk, and from its unique flame all other lights were taken to fill the church. 'The Blessing of the Fire and the Lighting of the Paschal Candle' is still observed ceremoniously in churches of the Roman communion and in some Anglican churches, for whom also the Easter carols are returning to life; † but we do not seem so far to have hit upon the obvious occasion for it: a Midnight Mass begun at a quarter to twelve in darkness. These candles descend from a custom much older than the Gospel in England. For on the same morning, in their own houses, the mediæval English were striking new fire, or 'need fire' as they called it, believing that unless all fires and lights were first put out, the straw would not catch. A couple of centuries ago it was still the custom "to do the fire out of the hall", clean all the smoke-blackened irons and fill the grate with flowers and branches. But that was more common before we altered our calendar; when the day became colder by nearly a fortnight.

The Feast of the Resurrection is by far the oldest of Christian festivals. We may be sure that there has never

* Thomas D. Fosbroke, *British Monachism*, 1802.
† See Appendix B.

[119]

been an 'Easter' unobserved since the original—and that is more than we would venture to claim for Christmas. In the little communities to whom St. Paul wrote letters of encouragement it was held to be the greatest day in the year. There do not seem to have been any Christian festivals distinct from the Jewish, but they kept the Passover "with the gladness of a new solemnity". Many believed that the world would end, one Easter or another: hence the gravity, and hence the joy. And while they looked for the Second Coming, some of them imagined this earth as it would be: not utterly destroyed—transformed rather—restored to the sharper reality of Eden; every created thing intensely glad to be none other than itself.

That is perhaps how the world may have seemed, for one moment, in the dawn of the original Easter. The full moon of the Passover appears to have set when Mary Magdalene entered the Garden in the darkness before day, and found the sepulchre wide open, and a figure of terrifying clarity. seated on the stone—or perhaps there were two figures inside: the accounts differ. Turning away from the empty tomb, and weeping then, she came face to face with another Presence, whom she addressed courteously as the gardener. Thus the Resurrection was revealed to a woman at sunrise, already accomplished, and the Church imagines it occurring at earliest dawn or cockcrow, which is another way of saying that mystically it does occur at that time.

But for mankind the portentous encounter took place "at the rising of the sun", and ever since, for that reason, men have gone out of doors to await the sunrise of Easter with excitement and joy. "Devout and holy Men," Bourne reminds us, "did in the best Ages of the Church, rise early in the Morning of the Resurrection. The Primitive Christians spent the Night preceding it, in Prayers and

Praises, till the Time of Cock-crow, the supposed Hour of our Saviour's rising. For it is universally assented to, that after our Saviour had conquer'd Death, and broken the Gates of Hell, he arose from the Dead, not at Mid-night, but at the Time of Cock-crow; which not the Cocks, but the Angels themselves proclaimed.   . Would we rise before the Sun, and prevent the Dawn of Day, our Meditations would be strong and vigorous, and almost persuade us that the real Actions of that Morn were presented to our View. For when at that Time all Things are husht in Silence, and wrap'd in Darkness, or but illuminated with the friendly Moon, the Guide of Mary Magdalene and the other Women to the Sepulchre, 'tis easy and natural to Meditate on these things."

Thus the contemplative in many ages: but the people looked for a sign. "It is a common Custom to rise before the Sun on Easter-day, and walk into the Fields to see the Sun *Dance;* which they have been told, from an old tradition, always Dances upon that Day"—dances on the horizon, that is, and if one should happen to observe his reflection in a pool of clear water that moment, one would see there the image of a dancing Lamb. Still, "to rise with the View of the Vulgar is foolish and ridiculous." The idea was derided by eighteenth-century rationalism for "an old, weak, superstitious error". Even Sir Thomas Browne, no hater of curious fancies, had included it among his *Vulgar Errors,* for "though we would willingly assent unto any *sympathetical Exultation,* yet cannot conceive therein any more than a *tropical Expression.* Whether any such Motion there were in that Day wherein Christ arised, Scripture hath not revealed, which hath been punctual in other Records, concerning *Solary Miracles;* and the Areopagite, that was amazed at the Eclipse, took no Notice of this." Undisturbed by these thoughts, many simple persons continued to climb the Wrekin and other high hills, believing they would see in that pale, bewildering eye the ecstatic image—never doubting the reality of a miracle; and at six in the morning, on the top of Yes Tor, it may well have appeared to have been affirmed.

Indeed, if the question were put: Does the sun dance or no?—both No and Yes could be given for an answer. On the plane of scientific accuracy, no. It may seem to, but this is a trick of the eyes. *That* kind of sun never dances: neither, for that matter, does it rise. But sympathetical Exultation may know that a different and more intimate sun does both rise and dance on the skyline of Easter. It is worth getting up to make trial of it.

"The Lord is risen!" The Easter greeting has a Russian sound. Yet we have heard that in the North a few country-people use it naturally enough, and being country-people they are less likely to have copied a Russian custom than to have inherited an English. From Adon, signifying Lord, both Adonis, the God of the Spring, and Adonai, the Supreme Being, derive their names. In the Risen Christ are consummated all previous sketches of the immortal victim, dead and reborn for the sake of men. All the beauty of early rejoicing is in harmony with Easter. The arum lilies in the wheelbarrow jolt their way to the shrine.

On the altar there can be only white and green: the white of Resurrection and the green of eternal life: arum lilies and narcissi, white as angels' flesh by an empty tomb, and the deep green of English or Irish yew, the one evergreen that belongs to Easter and to no other festival. Yew in a churchyard is an emblem of life, not of death. It is a pity that Romantic verse and vulgar opinion have attached the epithets 'gloomy' and 'funereal' to its vital and lustrous darkness. But the rule of white and green applies only to the altar.

EASTER

Anywhere else, in church or home, all flowers are in favour and it would be simple to celebrate Easter as charmingly as to-day we celebrate Christmas and the Harvest; for what profusion is offered! Primrose, moody violet and up-thrusting potent crocus; daffodil and the more magic wild daffodil; hyacinth and grape hyacinth; windflowers like an exercise in delicacy, and the anemones of the Holy Land, believed to be "the lilies of the field"; squills and jonquils and the pasque-flower; crooked blackthorn glorified, Star of Bethlehem, flowering currant in a cloud of tingling fragrance, apple blow and wild cherry; childish periwinkle and cuckoo-pint; and for a very late Easter, speedwell, and the gold-tasselled trophies of the oak.

Preparations for Christmas could be made at leisure in the long crescendo of Advent. There was a fast on the Eve, it is true, though little observed in recent centuries, but no day that resembled Good Friday, the sorrow preceding the joy, which gave to Easter its meaning and quality. Easter decorations were mostly begun on the day before, and that is perhaps one reason for their being skimped. A charming device can be made from the deserted nest of a blackbird or thrush, lined with moss, and thickly rimmed with flowers. If the face of the clock announced Christmas in a wreath of holly, it can now announce Easter in a lighter wreath.* Garlands and balls of flowers have been hung from ribbons, and paper bells and balls of the Christmas kind might be used, white, blue, yellow, or green; but not red, for red is unseasonable. It is curious that Chaucer, the poet of Spring, should so often refer to its "smalle flowers white and red", and seem to think nothing, in all that abundance, worthy of mention but the daisy.

* Transform the Kissing Bough of Christmas into an Easter garland.—
See p. 144.

The customs of Christmas extend fairly evenly throughout the day, with a tendency to rise to a climax in the evening. Easter on the other hand is notably a morning festival There is sunrise in its carols. *Hilariter! hilariter!* is the cry. It was not the Church who insisted that the faithful put on new clothes to receive the sacrament, but the pagan habit remained in force and is now not wholly disregarded, as the flower in the buttonhole, the gay dress and the frivolous hat may testify. After all, Merry England lies only a foot under Modern: here and there a crack may be found; and something comes up through the crack. On the breakfast table there are Easter Eggs, one for each member of the household. The egg was an object of wonder to primitive people, perfectly shaped and guarding its secret, the house of new life; and the Church found no objection to receiving it at a better altar. "Bless, O Lord, we beseech Thee, this Thy creature of eggs, that it may become a wholesome sustenance to Thy faithful servants, eating in thankfulness to Thee, on account of the Resurrection."—Pope Pius V appointed that prayer for the use of the English. In course of time these 'Paschal Eggs' became 'Pace Eggs'—the only name for them still in some parts of Northumberland.

To-day we observe the Easter Egg becoming the symbol of a symbol. In one popular form it is no more than the shape and shell of an egg, and that made of chocolate, stamped with mechanical ornament in low relief, or wound in red ribbon. Normally the same design appears on both sides of an egg; for the two halves were made in a single mould. Before the war there were eggs to be had in all sizes, from auk to thrush. The smallest resembled wild birds' eggs, pink and blue and clumsily stippled: these were of sugar with a centre of marzipan, and sometimes a clutch of them would be sold in a nest. Then there were the larger, pasteboard eggs that pulled apart to reveal a toy duckling, or perhaps in wealthier days a pair of silk stockings. These artificial eggs are all comparatively recent. *The Illustrated London News* observed their growing popularity in 1874, but earlier than the middle of the century they do not seem to have been known. It would be interesting—and at the same time an antidote to nostalgia for the past—to draw up a list of the improvements wrought by industry in the keeping of festivals. Artificial Easter Eggs, paper decorations at Christmas, the glass ornaments on the Christmas tree, the Victorian Valentine, indoor fireworks, and the present-day splendour of outdoor fireworks—we owe them all, in greater or less degree, to machine or laboratory, Victorian or modern methods of manufacture. And that is not to belittle the artistry they involve.

For all that, the true Easter Egg, the cheapest and the most delightful, remains what it has been, an egg—hen's, duck's or goose's—decorated at home. This might be worth our remembering to-day, when the artificial variety are hard to come by. There are several methods of decoration, all of them used in the present century. If an egg is boiled in the outer skins of an onion, it acquires a delicately mottled complexion. If strips of coloured rag are bound on instead, the effect is of marbled paper, but the dye, needless to say, must not be fast. Another traditional method is to draw on the shell with a white wax pencil or a piece of candle brought to a point, and then put the egg in the dye: the result is a white inscription on a coloured ground.*

But of all methods the best is one which happens to be among the oldest in England. The egg is boiled in the dye, from which it emerges a lustrous red or green or blue. A

* In Switzerland tiny leaves and flowers are bound to the egg before boiling in onion peel, to produce a mosaic of white on a ground of primrose yellow or deep mahogany.

E*

sharp steel point is then used to inscribe a design on the surface, by removing the colour and revealing the natural white of the shell underneath. This was the method used by the present writer to decorate the Easter Eggs here illustrated. He used a tool designed for engraving on glass in diamond-point, but the technique more nearly resembles that of scraper-board, and the tool for that kind of work can be bought in the form of a nib. If the eggs are meant to be kept they ought to be boiled very hard.* They were sometimes to be seen in the corner-cupboards of Georgian farmhouses, each egg in a tall ale glass, mementoes of Easters gone by. And how much older they are than the eighteenth century can be gathered from a document of the time of Edward I, from which it appears that four hundred eggs were bought for eighteen pence, to be boiled and stained, or covered with leaf of gold, and distributed to the Royal household.† All colours have been used, and the axiom that red is unseasonable has never applied to the eggs. Only the rich could afford the golden apples of the sun; others preferred them bright scarlet, in allusion to the Blood of Christ (though the Chinese were dyeing them scarlet nine hundred years before that Blood was shed). For the egg is life's emblem, and red is the colour of life.

It was not mere fancy that suggested a leaping hare in the design. The hare is thought to have been sacred to Éastre, and to the vernal deities in other lands. German children believed that the Easter Eggs were laid by hares, and French children were told that they ran to Rome to fetch them. In England the little sugared eggs, that resemble those of wild birds, are to this day hidden about the garden, or in the house if it rains, and the children who go seeking them are

* An egg engraved about 1860 is still in good condition.
† William Hone, *The Every-Day Book*, Vol. I, Col. 429.

EASTER EGGS

Photographs of ducks' eggs engraved by Laurence Whistler.
They are boiled in dye and engraved with a steel point.

almost ready to believe in the "Easter Hare" who left them, so conveniently, half-hidden in tussocks of grass or in clumps of daffodils. For them this game is the pleasantest part of Easter.

Only decadent children speak of the "Easter Bunny". Rabbits—humdrum, overcrowded plebs—are nothing to Éastre. But the hare, swift, lonely and patrician, has mystery still. To his skyline silhouette, his eternal craving for distance, there is pinned even now the last hope of some long-outmoded divinity.

If any traditional food is still eaten, apart from the mottled or marbled, sugar or chocolate, eggs on the breakfast table, it must be the lamb and mint sauce of an Easter dinner. That was believed at one time to be the principal dish of the Last Supper. Possibly a few confectioners continue to make the round spiced cakes of the day. Respect for the Jews gave us them, and also the tansy cake and the tansy pudding, still favourite dishes in 1860, according to Chambers: they stood for the bitter herbs of the Passover. On the other hand, contempt for the Jews encouraged us to attack our bacon with extra relish that Sunday. We liked to remember how the Hebrews ate, and also to laugh at them. Bourne says they were accustomed to eat "small fishes because of the Leviathan, and a hard egg because of the Bird Ziz".

Christ was crucified at the full moon of the Passover, and rose on the third day. If the early Church had allowed her principal fast and feast to follow the vagaries of the Paschal moon through March and April there would have been less trouble for us over dates. But she decided, at the Council of Nicaea in 325, that the Resurrection must be kept on a Sunday, and the Crucifixion on the Friday before. This means in effect that Easter may fall on any date between March 22nd and April 25th, including those dates.

If Easter is movable, it follows that all occasions governed by remoteness from Easter move with it, from Septuagesima Sunday nine weeks before, to Trinity Sunday eight weeks after it. In terms of this book, it means that Shrove Tuesday, Mothering Sunday, Palm Sunday, Good Friday, Rogationtide and Whitsun are early or late according to the incidence of Easter. The vagrancy of a public holiday could only cause distress and confusion in the modern world of affairs. Many businesslike persons consider it the height of whimsicality to derange the smooth running of an office for the sake of a full moon. Chambers of Commerce have been demanding a fixed Easter for over forty years. International appeals have been made—to the Holy See—to the League of Nations—and a good deal of sympathy has been found. In 1928 the third reading of an Act of Parliament was passed: Great Britain will keep Easter on the first Sunday after the second Saturday in April, if the rest of the world will consent to do the same. The world is likely to agree on a Sunday, sooner or later, and it may not be long before Appendix A of this book becomes irrelevant.

What can be said in opposition to the will of so many?— That the Paschal Moon is the glory of Passion Week? That Good Friday is not to be robbed of historic moonlight for the sake of convenience?—The moonlight is much; yet it might be best for the movable festivals if they did become stationary, or nearly so. Some of them are not very conspicuous in the modern world: they cannot afford to be elusive as well.

ST. GEORGE'S DAY

APRIL 23RD

Our ancient word of courage.
WILLIAM SHAKESPEARE—*Richard III*

SAINT of an English Army before he was Saint of England, St. George can have been a soldier, but no Englishman. Legends gathered about him early, and many writers, including Gibbon, confused him with a later and better-established George, Archbishop of Alexandria. The earlier Saint was an officer in the Roman army under Diocletian, who refused to abandon his faith during the Terror, and was martyred about the year 300—supposedly on April 23rd. In course of time he became the example of a Christian fighting-man, "the Great Martyr" as they called him in Greece, and the soldier-hero of the Middle Ages, of whom remarkable deeds were reported.*

In *The Golden Legend* of the thirteenth century, Jacobus de Voragine dealt with him handsomely. One day, according to that writer, St. George rode up to the heathen city of Sylene in Lybia, where he found the citizens in great distress. A neighbouring dragon had forced them to surrender two sheep each day for its dinner, and when the sheep gave out, two of their children; and now they were about to sacrifice the King's daughter, dressed as if for her wedding. St. George encountered the party by a stagnant lake, where the dragon lived, and finally induced the Princess to explain

* *Acta Sanctorum.*

[129]

her misery. At that moment the dragon appeared, inexpressibly revolting. The Saint charged, drove his spear into the gaping mouth, and to everyone's amazement tumbled the monster over and over. Then he persuaded the Princess to tie her girdle around its neck and lead it back to Sylene herself—a sight which not unnaturally emptied the city. When the inhabitants came timidly back, he promised to behead the dragon if they would all receive baptism. In this way over fifteen thousand souls were added to the faith; and four carts were commissioned to remove the body.

The Archangel Michael ejected a greater dragon from heaven, and some believe St. George to have been confounded with him. That would be a proof of his high renown. He became a symbol of the war against evil, and is usually portrayed trampling the dragon of sin under his horse's hoofs. Whether we should see in him a remoter symbol of Summer destroying Winter is open to speculation. Uncouth impersonators of Winter have been happily larruped out of villages, tumbled in ditches and pelted with mud, at this time of year, since village history began.

In 1098 our Norman soldiers were struggling under the walls of Antioch, hard put to it, when St. George appeared on his charger, like the Angels of Mons, and led the allied army to victory. Later he appeared again when the troops of Richard I were engaging the Saracens. The returning Crusaders brought with them their tale, and the battle-cry it resulted in; and presently England put herself under the protection of the Saint. His day was declared a holiday in 1222; and in his name Edward III founded the Order of the Garter, claimed to be the noblest brotherhood of knights in Europe: it preceded by many years the Order of St. Michael in France, of the Golden Fleece in Burgundy,

of St. Andrew in Scotland, and of St. George in the Holy
Roman Empire. Later the Knights acquired their Chapel at
Windsor, rebuilt on the King's orders in the name of their
Saint. They were originally the closest companions of the
King; in an age when he rode to battle, his chosen brothers-
in-arms. Later, a breath of politics rather dimmed their
glamour. Now, in 1946, the King has returned to choosing
his Knights without reference to any minister; and his
choice has fallen on the men in all three Services who chiefly
led us to victory.

The true birthday of the Order is not certainly known,
but it is said by some to have been St. George's Day, 1347.
The ceremonial was magnificently festive. "A white swan,
gorged or," was the device borne by the King himself; and
this the swaggering motto—"Hay, hay, the white swan:
By God's soul I am thy man."*

In this way did we learn "our ancient word of courage,
fair St. George". His was the name shouted, in Middle
English and Anglo-French, at numberless mediæval engage-
ments, to straighten the line or lead an attack, and
Shakespeare is fond of introducing these dramatic appeals
to his birthday Saint. An old injunction to the English
infantry declares:† "Item, that all souldiers entering into
battaile, assault, skirmish, or other faction of armes, shall
have for their common cry and word, *St. George forward*, or,
Upon them St. George, whereby the soldier is much comforted,
and the enemie dismaied by calling to minde the ancient
valour of England, which with that name has so often been
victorious." The Irishman, too, had been instructed in the
reign of Henry VII, ‡ "to call on St. George, or the name of his
Sovereign Lord, the King of England," and no longer to

* Article in the *D.N.B.*
† Robert Nares, *A Glossary*, 1822.
‡ John Brady, *Clavis Calendaria*, 1812.

bellow the word which came to him naturally, and aroused all his latent patriotism,—"Aboo!"

Under thistle, shamrock and leek, the Scotch, the Irish and the Welsh keep the day of their Saint with a fervour characteristic of small nations. The English are a little slack—but less so in the present century than in the last. By tradition, April 23rd is the day for a red rose in the buttonhole, the national flower. Unfortunately, the corrected calendar has made it more difficult to find a red rose at this early date; but fortunately, on the other hand, the forcing of flowers out of season has made it easier. A modest revival of St. George's Day began in the last years of the old century, and by the 1930's appeared to have made some progress. Many towns and villages remembered the day; a service might be held, or the children given a holiday, and flags and roses were to be seen. Sometimes a pageant has formed part of a flower show or fête, with a Saint and a Dragon, and other, extraneous characters. Here it would be wrong to see nothing but antiquarian sentiment at work. Village festivals are old, whether they mark the dedication day of the church, or this holiday, at one time general. Sometimes fireworks have brightened the end of St. George's Day, as at the Chester Races in 1610.* Summer is the season for fireworks in England, and we enter Summer— symbolically at least—on the first of May. Yet the evenings of late April are often warm enough for an entertainment of this kind.

A red cross on a white field, the flag of St. George may fly from the church tower, not only on St. George's Day, but whenever a parish keeps festival. To replace it with the Union Jack is quite incorrect on these occasions. The Union Jack is the flag of the United Kingdom. It denotes

* See p. 171.

the union of four countries and the pomp of Empire, but it is not the flag of England nor the flag of the English Church. Simpler and lovelier are the emblems of St. George, that belong to the towers they have crowned and the landscape they have touched with heraldic gaiety for so many Aprils. They are English like "Early One Morning", the turrets of Hampton Court, or the words of the Communion Service.

Shakespeare was born, it is pleasant to suppose, on April 23rd, 1564, and he died on the same day in 1616. The festival at Stratford-on-Avon each year is the most cosmopolitan in character of any we keep.   Foreign ambassadors arrive by train; flagpoles are set up along Bridge Street; and at noon the flags of the nations are unfurled. Pilgrimages are made to the birthplace and the grave, and the town is full of strangers—Chinese, Arabians, Indians, Americans—as well as of scholars, actors, poets, antiquarians and trippers.   Some of the visitors bring cowslips and primroses to lay on the stone.   The celebration of "the Birthday" is now the main feature of St. George's Day, and though the connexion may be accidental, there are many who have it in mind.   It is curious that the greatest of Englishmen may have entered and left this world, at the same place in the heart of England, on the festival of England's guardian Saint.

MAY DAY

MAY 1ST

For what clipping, what culling, what kissing and bussing, what smouching and slabbering one of another, is not practiced every wher at these dauncings? All which, whether they blow up Venus' cole or not, who is so blind that seeth not?

PHILIP STUBBES—*Anatomie of Abuses*, 1583

AGAINST May," continues the author of that well-nourished Anatomy, "all the yung men and maides, old men and wives, run gadding over night to the woods, groves, hils, and mountains, where they spend all the night in plesant pastimes; and in the morning they return, bringing with them birch and branches of trees, to deck their assemblies withall. And no mervaile, for there is a great Lord present amongst them, as superintendant and Lord over their pastimes and sportes, namely, Sathan, prince of hel. But the chiefest iewel they bring from thence is their May-pole, which they bring home with great veneration, as thus. They have twentie or fortie yoke of oxen, every Oxe having a sweet nose-gay of flowers placed on the tip of his hornes, and these oxen draw home this May-pole (this

[134]

stinkyng Ydol, rather) which is covered all over with floures and hearbs, bound round about with strings from the top to the bottome, and sometime painted with variable colours, with two or three hundred men, women and children following it with great devotion. And thus being reared up, with handkercheefs and flags hovering on the top, they straw the ground rounde about, binde green boughes about it, set up sommer haules, bowers, and arbours hard by it; and then fall they to daunce about it, like as the heathen people did at the dedication of the Idols, whereof this is a perfect pattern, or rather the thing itself. I have heard it credibly reported (and that *viva voce*) by men of great gravitie and reputation, that of fortie, threescore, or a hundred maides going to the wood over night, there have scarcely the third part of· them returned home againe undefiled."

Stubbes would not have been at all surprised to have learnt that the Old Saxons, long before they invaded this country, had actually worshipped a Maypole at Marsburg in North Germany, an immense emblematic contraption called by them 'Irminsul'.*

The pagan character of May Day had always been well understood by a few, and the Protestant reformers were by no means the first to denounce the loose living it sometimes occasioned. But until the reign of Queen Elizabeth there had been no strong body of English opinion opposed to the keeping of festivals in a decent manner. Secular authority had always approved of the May. One year the poet Lydgate had sent a May poem to the Aldermen and Sheriffs of London "being on May Day at the Bishop of London's Wood, and having there a worshipful Dinner for them-

---

*The word signifies "enormous pillar". It was pulled down by Charlemagne's order in 772. H. M. Chadwick, *The Origin of the English Nation*, 1907, Chap. X.

selves".* The fifteenth century author of *The Court of Love* described a more romantic outing—

> And furth goth all the Court, both most and lest,
> To feche the floures fresh, and braunche and blome;
> And namly, hawthorn brought both page and grome,
> With fresch garlandes, partie blewe and whyte
> Eke eche, at other threw the floures bright,
> The prymerose, the violet, the gold.

This happened in the Court of Cupid, yet the poet knew well that even courtiers of flesh and blood would get up early to bring in the May. When peace prevailed in England this frequently happened. Henry VIII went maying on many occasions. One year, early in the morning, he and Queen Catherine of Aragon, with a large number of attendants, rode from Greenwich to the top of Shooter's Hill, "where, as they passed by the way, they espyed a company of tall yeomen, clothed all in greene, with greene hoods, and with bowes and arrowes, to the number of two hundred. One, being then chieftaine, was called Robin Hood, who required the King and all his company to stay and see his men shoot."† No doubt the King had expected something of the kind. Robin Hood was already the representative figure of 'Old England'. The party drew rein, and then, at a word from their captain, the two hundred bowmen loosed together. Each arrowhead had been made to whistle in flight, like a present-day whistling rocket, "so that the noise was strange and loud, which greatly delighted the king, queene, and their company—Moreover this Robin Hood desired the king and queene, with their retinue, to enter the greene wood, where, in arbours made of boughes, and deckt with

* See John Stow, *Survey of London*, 1598, for this and the following anecdote of Henry VIII.
† Quoted by William Hone, *The Every-Day Book*, Vol. I, Col. 550-2.

flowers, they were set and served plentifully with venison and wine, by Robin Hood and his meyny, to their great contentment, and had other pageants and pastimes."

Meanwhile the King's humbler subjects might have been seen, with boughs in their hands, and wreaths of marigolds and windflowers about their foreheads, straggling homeward across the pastures, or crowded together about some object of trembling leaves and flowers that they were dragging towards the town. They had been out since midnight, or longer, even as Stubbes reported, losing themselves by groups and couples in the dark rain-warm thickets, hearing all round them laughter and the snapping of twigs, shouts from wood to wood, hooting on horns, or the twang of a stringed instrument. At earliest bird-song they had begun tearing the hawthorn, before they could well see it, and now, with the sun, they were turning homewards to garnish their doors and windows. Presently there would be dancing on the green, with archery and vaulting; and when night fell there might be bonfires in the streets—the Beltane fires once common in the North and the West.*

The Puritans accused the clergy of condoning these frivolities and even of sponsoring the more innocent kind on the village green. Many of them undoubtedly did, and saw no harm in it, either. If May Day fell on a Sunday, that was not thought to raise any serious difficulty. The wandering musicians arrived as usual, and the people simply moved between church and green, first to compulsory Matins, and then to dancing and feasting; then perhaps to daylight Evensong, and then to dancing once more—on into the twilight, till the fiddler was tuning up afresh in the alehouse,

* Beltane was the Celtic name for the great Fire Festival of May 1st. The incident on Mount Carmel has led to a false derivation. The word has no connexion with Bel or Baal of the Old Testament. It is doubtful if the ritual fires were ever a great feature of Anglo-Saxon May Day.

bowls and ropes and targets being gathered away, "and sport no more seen on the darkening Green."

Among the dancers and wrestlers, the archers and runners, had moved the parson, pausing here to admire the ripple of biceps, or there, like Robert Herrick, to scrutinise the girls; sanctioning all they did by his presence, even if dignity whispered that he ought not to join in the woven measures himself. (But sometimes he did.)

He had the support of the government, if not of the local magistrates; since one of the "lawful recreations" for a Sunday afternoon, mentioned in King James's *Book of Sports*, had been "the setting up of May Poles".* That book caused offence, and a rebellious Parliament was glad to revoke its orders. In 1644 Christmas and May Day were abolished together. An Ordinance forbad the "prophanation of the Lord's Day by May Poles (a heathenish vanity generally abused to superstitution and wickedness). All and singular May Poles", it declared, "shall be taken down and removed by the constables and church wardens of the parishes   and, that no May Pole shall be hereafter set up within this Kingdom of England or dominion of Wales, the said officers to be fined five shillings weekly till the said May Pole be taken down."†

This order implies that the Maypole was more often a permanent fixture than a tree dragged in from the wood by oxen with flower-tipped horns. Perhaps the same had been true before the Saxon invasion. There may have been other and smaller Irminsuls North of the Elbe, and in places where none had been erected the people may have found a substitute in the wood, or danced about a living tree stuck full of flags or ribbons, in the way their descendants would dance

---

* See Introduction, p. 12.

† *Acts and Ordinances of the Interregnum.*

about the Appleton Thorn in Cheshire. But the permanent
pole was surely more common in any period. The "Lostock
mepul" is mentioned in the reign of King John.* Tall as a
modest church tower, and sometimes taller—so lofty was
one in the mediæval City that a church nearby became known
as St. Andrew *Undershaft*—it generally stood throughout the
year, sometimes painted in spiral bands, red and white, like
a barber's pole; to be dressed every May Day in garlands of
flowers twisted about it, and in flying ribbons and flags.

Of the poles that came down in the Commonwealth many
were put up again at the Restoration. In very remote places
a few may have stood where they were, undisturbed though
unregarded, till a better climate returned. "The happiest
Mayday that hath been many a year in England"—that was
how Pepys described the first of King Charles's reign. He
had in mind a symbolic ceremony that had taken place in
the Strand that day, before a big crowd of approving
Londoners. A truly prodigious Irminsul had been erected
in the middle of the street, just where its humble predecessor had been felled, a site now occupied by the
charming 'island' church of St. Mary. It was no less than
134 feet high: made in two parts "below bridge", and floated
up stream to Scotland Yard, whence it was conveyed along
Whitehall with military music and "multitudes of people
thronging the streets, with great shouts and acclamations all
day long". Twelve seamen, used to handling tackle, were
employed in the erecting, and as it rose from the ground,
trumpets broke into a fanfare. Four hours later it was firm,
and then again there was a fanfare and a shout that echoed
along the Strand. Surmounting the pole was a crown with the
royal arms riding golden, and a purple streamer. About the
middle were four more crowns, and then a garland of many

* Sir William Dugdale, *Monasticon Anglicanum*, 1896, Vol. 6, Pt. 2, p. 907.

[139]

colours, and below that again three lanterns, to be lit at nightfall as long as the pole existed. It was a great ornament, and a useful one; and before the apprentices had finished gaping, the Morris men had appeared waving their purple scarves and moving to "the ancient Musick".

Most careful is the author of *Cities Loyally Displayed* in 1661 to affirm that all was as it used to be—only better, of course—the same music and the same situation: "as near as they could guess, in the very same pit where the former stood." Old England returning to herself was the meaning of the symbol. "Little children did much rejoice, and antient people did clap their hands, saying, golden days began to appear. I question not but 'twill ring like melodious musick throughout every county in England." Yet, in a manner quite unforeseen, the Restoration had a limiting effect on May Day observance. A rival event had been found in Oak Apple Day, falling on the 29th, when the return of the King was celebrated. This popular day stole the honours and many of the customs from the earlier festival. But the Stuart glory was not to remain so bright; and thus, at the beginning of King George's reign, both festivals were decaying.* The highest Maypole in history disappeared from view in another symbolic hour. In 1717 Sir Isaac Newton took it away to support the most modern and powerful telescope in the world.

No one could look with a fresher eye at May Day in Regency England than Washington Irving. He had never seen a Maypole till he came to this country. He was an American, born of English parents, greatly pleased by English customs. He formed the opinion that May Day was

* In the 1890's, many railway engines of the Manchester, Sheffield and Lincolnshire Railway were decorated with boughs of oak on Oak Apple Day. Now it is largely forgotten, and there seems to be no good reason for wishing to revive it, in a month which frequently contains both May Day and Whitsun.

dying here, and that little would come of attempts to revive it. He wrote of the dancing and pageantry as already things of the past. There is nothing remarkable in this except that precisely the same opinion might be formed by a casual observer now. May Day appears, at first sight, to have stood still for a hundred and thirty years. It cannot be said to have recovered very greatly, but on the other hand, if it dies it dies very slowly.

The present state of the May Festival is rather ambiguous, and its future more than usually difficult to predict. When it had almost ceased to mean anything, it gained a new and quite different meaning. It became Labour Day, chosen in 1889 by the first Congress of the Second International at Paris—presumably because it remained, on the Continent, very much a *people's* day, and one which owed little or nothing to the Church. The workers were told to enforce a holiday, no matter what the day of the week, and bloodshed was often the result. In peaceable England, Labour Day is generally kept on the first Sunday in the month, and in London the traditional gathering place is Hyde Park. Socialist writers of the William Morris school were pleased to imagine a link with the older festival, and Walter Crane's cartoons of the early '90's heroically supported the idea.* We see a political Maypole, the workers dancing about it, men and girls, and to every streamer a slogan—"eight hours," "Leisure for all."—But in fact the two kinds of assembly had little in common; the one gaily traditional, the other grimly original. So it must be wherever a Socialist state is a hope and not an achievement. But once it comes into being the character of Labour Day unavoidably alters. While there is less of anger about it, there is, or there ought to be, more of joy. That would appear to be true of

* Victoria and Albert Museum collection.

Russia at the present time. Many peoples compose the Union of Socialist Soviet Republics, and we are told that the central government likes them to preserve their harmless differences. National costumes and dances are approved, and the Russians have not forgotten, as we so nearly have, how to sing the traditional songs. In this atmosphere some of the old May ritual is likely to survive.

We may perhaps see foreshadowed in Russia a fusion that will take place in England—if she is destined to become, in her own manner, a Socialist state. But it will be less apparent in England, where the countryman is not a peasant, and only the children are unselfconscious enough to dance in public. This many of them are now encouraged to do. It is evidently time to examine more closely Washington Irving's prediction, which for half a century appeared to be accurate enough. Chambers wrote in 1862: "Now alas! the May-pole has again vanished. They must be pretty old people who remember ever seeing one"—while he thought "the enthroning of the May Queen has been longer obsolete than even the May-pole". He would have been surprised to know that in the 1930's there would still be villages where the Maypole would be danced about,* and still a great many schoolchildren in London and the country who would keep the festival and crown a Queen. In the last fifty years there has been, in fact, a revival of interest in the May, but not so general that we can be sure it will last. It has to be remembered that there is, properly speaking, no *ancient* Maypole in existence. The great one in the Strand lasted for half a century, but that was exceptional. Normally they rot at the foot, and need to be renewed every fifteen years. The fact that quite a number are standing on traditional sites, and used

* See George Long, *The Folklore Calendar*, 1930; also A. R. Wright and T. E. Lones, *British Calendar Customs: England*, 1936–8, Vol. II, for recent examples of May observance given in this chapter.

by the children, is itself a proof of periodic revival.* Tennyson
perhaps began it, with his popular poem; William Morris
carried it on; the explorers and exponents of traditional songs
and dances gave it substance, and the Scouts and Guides translated it into action; but Ruskin is the man above all to whom
we owe the children's May Day. It was he who initiated the
'Coronation' ceremony at Whitelands College in the 1880's,
and all that followed can be traced back to him by way of
the young teachers from Whitelands.

Sunrise at Easter, but on May Day earliest dawn. To be
out of doors, even once in a country childhood, at the dark
hour when the birds reopen the Spring is a memorable
experience. According to ancient belief—a superstition,
but a harmless one—nothing makes beautiful like kissing
the dew on May morning. People have held that belief in the
present century. As for Mrs. Pepys in an earlier one, she
thought it "the only thing in the world to wash her face
with", and got up every year at four o'clock to do it. Some
used even to run a silver spoon through the grass, and bottle
it. Ignorant fancy!—yet a child would be a dullard that
could poke her chin in the crystals on a single leaf—each
with a microcosmic sunrise—and not learn anything fresh
about dew.

There are no oxen with flower-tipped horns, but there
are still cowslips and lilac, apple blossom and bluebells to
bring into the house, and in some families the children have
brought their parents a May bunch on this morning. Now
the morning comes eleven days sooner by the sun than it
came to Chaucer and Herrick, and eleven Spring days can

* The tallest to-day is probably the Maypole at Pagan Hill, Stroud, which
stands over eighty feet high. The pole at Welford-on-Avon is about seventy
feet. Those at Ilmington, Warwickshire, and Barwick-in-Elmet, Yorkshire,
are also very tall, and all four are traditionally placed.

alter the look of England. Wild roses and the may itself, the flower of the hawthorn, are seldom in time. Both were formerly used, and there appears to be nothing historical about the may superstition: that it brings bad luck into a room with its hot and crowding smell; for on the contrary, it was thought to keep ghosts away. There is evidently here a confusion of ideas. Late generations had an inkling that the tree was sacred, even before the Crown of Thorns had been woven. The sacred and the magical were not far apart. It was thought unlucky—and still is by some—to *cut down* a thorn, but never unlucky to rob it for the festival of Spring.

Of all May garlands—and there are many—the cowslip ball is the simplest to make. The many-branched heads of the flowers are cut off and stood along a string or ribbon, held taut, then carefully pressed toward the centre as the knot is tied. The completed ball can hang from a bow, or crown the tip of a peeled willow-wand. But the loveliest hanging garlands have a form already familiar to the reader of this book. One is made of intersecting circles of wire, concealed in blossom, a floral globe with a cowslip ball in the centre, or a gold and a silver ball representing the sun and the moon—a diagram of Spring in the Solar System. Another takes the form of a hemisphere or crown. These garlands are clearly nothing other than the Kissing Bough of Christmas translated into vernal language. Indeed, the same framework of wire—globe or crown—could be hung up at two or three festivals, and conceivably was, in the past: with apples and candles at Christmas; with flowers and eggs at Easter or May Day; and with corn at the Harvest.

Sometimes two circles, intersecting and bound with blossom, were fixed to the top of a staff, wound spirally with flowers in the manner of the classical thyrsus. In Rutland, before the war, garlands of the kind were made by children very early in the morning, from flowers they had picked on the evening before. The same device may well have been used at the Floralia in Roman Britain, the festival of Flora, goddess of flowers, heralded in Rome with a braying of trumpets. For Roman remains have been found in the neighbourhood of King's Lynn, and here, in the last century, these formal emblems were carried about the town with a great deal of monotonous hooting on cows' horns. The two large hoops were crossed on the point of a staff, and bound with bunches of flowers interspersed with evergreens. Wild birds' eggs were blown, threaded and looped in festoons from the top, and above them were bright-coloured flying ribbons. Below, on the centre of the globe, was a doll fixed to the top of the staff, her name long since forgotten. It may have been Flora herself. It was certainly the local goddess of flowers.*

This custom, too, would seem to have survived the wreck of the Roman province. At Horncastle in Lincolnshire, where the Maypole stood there was formerly a Roman temple, and the boys of the town continued to move in procession towards it, carrying wands of willow with the bark stripped away, and with chains of cowslips twisted about them. The wand, florally tipped or twisted, was everywhere much in use. So were the coronets, chains and cushions of flowers. Occasionally there were crosses, made of clipped yew or wood, decorated with bluebells and cuckoo-pints. It is worthy of remark that no May Day custom or emblem of a Christian kind has been mentioned before in this chapter. May is Mary's month in the Roman Church, as the schoolchildren know who process every Sunday in white satin and blue; but in the English Church the first of May is quite

* Illustrated in William Hone's *Table Book*, 1827, Pt. I. Rather similar garlands were made at Fontmell Magna in the 1930's—Rolf Gardiner, *England Herself*, 1943, p. 137.

unflorally dedicated to St. Philip and St. James. All the same, the redemption of May Day went further than is commonly supposed. As Spenser records in *The Shepherd's Calendar*, the young people returned from the woods to garnish, not only their doors and windows, but—

> all the Kirke pillours eare day-light,
> With Hawthorne buds, and sweete Eglantine,
> And girlonds of roses, and Sopps in wine,

—sufficient proof that the buds of the may were not then thought to be unlucky. That was a long time ago; but there remains the hymn at sunrise on the top of the Bargate at Southampton, and the better known service on the top of Magdalen Tower at Oxford, where at six in the morning the choir are heard, by a large crowd in the street below, singing "*Te Deum Patrem colimus*". The ritual is thought by some to be a great deal older than the tower, and a great deal older than the requiem mass once said each year, for the soul of Henry VII, on the tower roof. The sun, the father of life as men saw him, was commonly worshipped in high places. Akhenaten and Nefertiti went up a tower to adore the sunrise, and to receive on their lips and eyelids the fingertips and ankhs of felicity, stretched out to them by the first horizontal beams.

The service over, Magdalen bells ring out and the Morris men appear, dancing in the streets. Christian May Day— curious though the epithet sounds—has a certain substance in the neighbourhood of Oxford. At Cowley, in the present century, the children have brought bunches of flowers to church. At Charlton-on-Otmoor a wooden cross above the screen is still, apparently, decorated by children on May Day, and the children have made little replicas for themselves, which they show for a penny. They will sing, then, one of the old May Carols; and of these there were several versions alive, in various parts of England, during the 1930's. One of the most charming used to be known as 'The Mayers' Song':*

Remember us poor Mayers all,
  And thus do we begin
To lead our lives in righteousness
  Or else we die in sin.

We have been rambling all this night,
  And almost all this day,
And now returned back again
  We have brought you a branch of May.

A branch of May we have brought you,
  And at your door it stands,
It is but a sprout, but it's well budded out
  By the work of our Lord's hands.

The hedges and trees they are so green,
  As green as any leek,
Our heavenly Father He watered them
  With his heavenly dew so sweet.

The heavenly gates are open wide,
  Our paths are beaten plain,
And if a man be not too far gone,
  He may return again.

The life of man is but a span,
  It flourishes like a flower.
We are here to-day, and gone to-morrow,
  And we are dead in an hour.

* Music and slightly inferior words in *The Oxford Book of Carols*, by Percy Dearmer and Vaughan Williams, Nos. 48 and 49.

> The moon shines bright, and the stars give a light,
>   A little before it is day,
> So God bless you all, both great and small,
>   And send you a joyful May.

There is something of sadness about it, both words and tune, as about all purely sensuous joy; for May Day is not Easter, and the joys it has known have always been earth-bound, blind and fleeting.

Christianity has acquired another primeval custom. At Tissington in Derbyshire, as at Wirksworth about Whitsun, there are placed in certain well-heads, with a brief service on a May morning which crowds of visitors attend, bright elaborate pictures very curiously contrived. They are made out of flower-petals, moss, lichen, berries, and other minutiæ stuck on wet clay, which enables them to keep their vividness for several days. The subject is normally a sacred one, and over the top may be written in grains of rice, "Praise the Lord." These mosaics are delightfully executed, and sometimes have the childish charm of an old Staffordshire or Swansea picture-plate. The custom is purely local, and so is the much-reported Furry Dance of Helston in Cornwall, an Iberian or Celtic survival, and without doubt the best example in modern times of a whole community given over to May celebration. For the Holiday is general. At five or six, green boughs are brought home and the houses decorated. At seven there is dancing in the street to the Helston tune—

> And we were up as soon as any day O
> And for to fetch the Summer home.

About ten the children dance with wands of willow, and at noon the town officials lead off in the "Invitation Dance", the

THE SPIRIT OF MAY DAY.
From a fifteenth century MS. in the British Museum.

men in top hats and morning suits, the women in their smartest dresses. Following the band, they dance through the narrow streets; they bow and curtsey to bring one another the "Summer"; where they find shut doors they knock on them; where doors are open they dance right through the houses and out at the back.* This curious survival appears to refute the statement that May Day is only enjoyed by the children now. Perhaps the carnival is too well attended to cause embarrassment. After all, it is not the breaking of conventions, but the being observed while doing so, that embarrasses. What finally chills the heart of even the sprightliest Morris lady is nothing but a row of glum faces along the wall.

But in the end we must return to the London Elementary School Children—we must catch them while they are still busy with multicoloured ribbons at Blackheath, and before they have given thought to red flags in Trafalgar Square. Theirs are now the arbour and the crowning of the Queen, the garlands on poles and the Maypole crowned with St. George's flag. They will take out the streamers that hang from it in a wide circle, they will bow to one another, and move off to a lilting tune, half with the sun and half against it, weaving in and out, drawn closer to the centre by the shortening streamers, till, the tune changing, they turn face about, and set off again to unravel the plaited pole. It is all very innocent, and rather a long way from the hot-blooded welcome to Summer that Philip Stubbes blasted with appropriate gusto.†

In evolving a May pageant for children there are many

* See Christina Hole, *English Custom and Usage*, 1941. The carnival is kept on May 8th, and appears to have altered little in a century. It concludes with a Ball at night.

† The crowning of a child Queen, the dwarf Maypole and the ribbon-plaiting dances were all introduced or inspired by Ruskin, and formed no part of the ancient festival, where a 'Lord' and a 'Lady' presided, the Maypole was large, and the dances were by grown men or youths.

F

traditional features other than those already described, worthy of a moment's consideration. There is the Green Man, or Jack-in-Green, a figure entirely hidden to his shoes within a cone of leaves and flowers fastened to a frame, a walking obelisk to Flora. Thus he appeared at Knutsford in Cheshire, in 1938. Once a part of the chimney-sweepers' frolic, Jack-in-Green was thought by Chambers, quite wrongly, to be the last surviving feature of a London May Day.*

Perhaps the best pageant would be a very ancient one: the Battle of Winter and Summer. At first Winter is discovered in possession of the field. He appears to be a very old man with wild hair and beard, clothed all in furs, and the sceptre in his hand is a leafless branch. All his dingy courtiers are brandishing bare branches: there must be no evergreens here, no hint of Father Christmas; for here there is Winter absolute, without hope of rebirth. They are entertaining him with the 'rough music' he likes: with beating on metal, jangling of chains, shrill blasts and siren wails. Then, distantly, another music is heard, the music of instruments and voices, where the army of Summer approaches with dancing. Some carry flower-tipped wands and garlands on poles. Some are scattering leaves and petals in the path of Flora. A mock battle ensues and Winter is driven from the field, his sceptre seized and twined with flowers, and presented to the Queen as she ascends her throne.

---

* See p. 172. Mention must also be made of the Milkmaids' garland, though it is not likely to be seen any more: a glittering trophy of silver utensils, fixed to a cloth-covered pyramid, carried about like a sedan chair on poles. (Illustration in *The Every-Day Book*, col. 570.) In London, before the war, a few horses might be seen with ribbons to their harness, an old May custom, handsomely kept in Liverpool.

ROGATIONTIDE

THE FIFTH WEEK AFTER EASTER WEEK*

For this cause be certaine Gospels red in the wide fieldes amonges the corne and grasse.

Old Sermon

WHEN a Christian custom of modern England is derived from a heathen custom of ancient Rome, it is very unlikely that the Roman British passed it on to the hated barbarians. A hint of some Roman grace may have lingered in the May Day garlands of King's Lynn, where perhaps the enslaved British were allowed to do as they had always done—the Nordic god was not a jealous god—; but instances of the kind are few and doubtful. Where the elements fused are Christian and Latin-pagan (as opposed to Nordic-) the fusion can only have occurred in the Latin South. The custom must then have come in with the foreign priests, who found it easy to implant if a clumsy native equivalent already existed.

So it must have been with the ritual observed in Rogation week. According to the Acts of the Apostles, Christ remained on earth for forty days after the Resurrection, and on the fortieth ascended into heaven. But the custom kept by the peoples of the West on Holy Thursday, or one of the days immediately before it, does not reflect the Ascension at all. Two festivals of the Roman world occurred at this season: the Terminalia and the Ambarvalia. When the

* See Appendix A.

Romans thought of the god Terminus they did not see him in the shape of a man; his statue was merely the boundary stone or wooden post between properties. An animal had bled to death at the setting up of it, and every year thereafter the two neighbouring landlords visited the statue together to crown it with garlands, while renewing the sacrifice. But this they did towards the end of February, and that is a long time before Ascension Day. The influence of the Ambarvalia, falling in May, must surely have been greater: Rome herself kept it on the 29th, at a certain place in the old perimeter of Roman territory. Here a crowd assembled to move in procession around the corn-fields, with singing and dancing, the sacrifice of animals, the driving away of Winter with sticks, and other enjoyable rites, intended to rid the cornlands of evil. Country people are stubborn about losing their customs, but do not object to keeping them for a better reason, or even on a different day. About the year 465 the Western world was suffering from earthquake, storm and epidemic. Mamertus, Bishop of Vienne, aware of the popular custom, ordered that prayers should be said in the ruined or neglected fields on Ascension Day or the three days preceding it. 'Beating the Bounds' had become a Christian ceremonial.

It was introduced into England early in the eighth century, and has remained with us ever since. During Rogationtide, at any period in history, including our own, a party might be seen setting out to trace the boundaries of the parish. At the head marched the bishop or the priest, with a minor official bearing the Cross, and after them followed a crowd of persons, including the schoolboys of the parish, led by their master. Most of them held slender wands of willow, like those of May Day, peeled white, and sometimes crowned, a little below the top, with a knot of flowers. At certain points along the route, at certain well-known land-marks—bridge or stile, or oftenest an ancient tree—the Cross halted, the party gathered about the priest, and a litany or rogation was said, imploring God to send seasonable weather, keep the corn and the roots and the boughs in good health, and bring them to an ample harvest. At one point beer and cheese would be waiting, provided out of small endowments made for that purpose. A rogation is no more than an 'asking', appropriate to any emergency, war, plague, drought or foul weather. The heathen perambulations of Spring had merely suggested a rogation of a fixed and perennial sort.

Then, beneath the "Gospel Oak", or at the boulder on the hill, a curious duty was performed. The wand-bearers set to work to beat the landmark with their clashing wands. Suddenly, amid shouts of amusement, they transferred their attack to one of the boys, who offered himself, half-willing and half-reluctant. They rolled him in a briar bush, flung him in a pond, or, seizing him by shoulders and heels, bumped him several times against the boundary stone. Though lucky to escape without a scratch, a bruise or a wetting, the sacrificial victim did not show any great reluctance, for a new shilling was likely to be his reward. The Church will hardly have invented such a custom, and here we must surely see an element introduced by the Saxon peoples themselves, who are known to have had their vernal "gang days", resembling, however roughly, the rites of the South.

In the days when maps were neither common nor accurate there was much to be said for this antiquated form of field punishment. The sufferer was not likely to forget the duckweed he had swallowed or the nettles that had brailled his cheeks. If ever the parish boundaries came into dispute, there would be some old man in the alehouse with a warm remembrance of the field in question. But in fact they can seldom have been disputed; for these perennial marches— common still in the reign of Queen Victoria—fixed the geography of the parish in the mind of everyone present, and opportunity was taken to rebuild the tumbled landmark, if that should be necessary.

For the larger purpose of the ceremony let us listen to what George Herbert tells us in *The Country Parson*. Clergymen, he says, ought to encourage it for four reasons:

1. A blessing of God for the fruits of the field.
2. Justice, in the preservation of bounds.
3. Charitie, in loving walking and neighbourly accompanying one another, with reconciling of differences at that time, if they be any.
4. Mercie, in relieving the poor by a liberal distribution of largess, which at that time is or ought to be used.

Isaac Walton tells us that Richard Hooker—stout landmark himself of the reformed Church—was of the same opinion, "persuading all, both rich and poor, if they desired the preservation of love, to accompany him in his Perambulation: and most did so: in which Perambulation he would usually express more pleasant discourse than at other times, and would always drop some loving and facetious observations, to be remembered against the next year, especially by the boys and young people."

Beating the bounds fell off in the last century, like greeting the May, and like that too, although for a different reason, is somewhat revived. The Churches hold it their duty to "go out into the fields" again, and not into the fields merely, but into the streets and factories, because, in the words of M. Maritain, "One of the worst vices of the modern world is its dualism, the dissociation between the things of God and the things of the world. The latter, the things of social, economic and political life, have been abandoned to their own carnal law, removed from the exigencies of the Gospel. The result is that they have become increasingly unlivable."[*] There is more to this "going out", we presume, than physically going out with a banner and a handful of choir boys, whose bottoms are now no longer in danger; but the ceremony has a part to play in the greater scheme. Now, in the country, it is more a case of blessing the fields than of beating the bounds; there is no good reason to-day for walking all round a country parish; instead, the procession moves from one kind of territory to another: to bless the corn, the pastures, the fruit trees and gardens, and at the river's brink the waters.

In this modern, workaday world with very few holidays, the minor festivals tend to escape from the working week and fasten themselves on the nearest week-end; or perhaps it would be truer to say that, industry having squeezed them to death, those who begin to revive them would certainly fail if they were sticklers in the matter of dates. Plough Monday has largely withdrawn in favour of Plough Sunday; May Day, at school, is often the nearest Saturday; Lammas becomes the first Sunday in August; and even the Harvest Thanksgiving begins to be held on a Sunday. The development is natural enough, and Rogationtide demonstrates it too. The crops used to be blessed on the Monday, Tuesday, Wednesday or Thursday, and the chosen day was a holiday. Now the custom is generally kept on the Sunday before. The dioceses of Chichester, Lincoln and Salisbury have each issued a temporary service, and on the experience gained in

[*] *Scholasticism and Politics*, trans. Adler, 1945, p. 17.

those and other parts of the country, the Council for the Church and Countryside are drafting an authorised form of worship.* In his pastoral letter of 1944 the Bishop of Chichester invited the Sussex countryman "to observe Rogation Sunday, now happily chosen by the Minister of Agriculture as Farm Sunday". It has been found since then that a farmer rather enjoys reading the Gospel aloud in his own pastures.

The custom, in its older form, might well be encouraged for another and purely social reason. We deplore Victorian brickwork, yet England has suffered more damage at the hands of the selfish, the ignorant, and the mercenary-minded in the present century than ever before. Government action has little effect if it lacks the support of a fully alert and intelligent public opinion. Unfortunately most Englishmen who live in cities, or near them, know extraordinarily little about their immediate neighbourhood. Too busy to examine it carefully, they spend their holidays on other ground. But is it fanciful to suppose that if a number of children were to explore their parish thoroughly, one or two of them would remain awake to the changes afterwards proposed in it, for better or worse? Town parishes are small, as a rule, and the boundaries moderately near at hand, if peculiarly difficult to find. The custom revived before the war in the London parish of St. Clement Danes deserves to be noted. The clergy and choir assemble at the church and set out in procession, with a beadle carrying the mace. Rosettes are worn, and the schoolboys who accompany the procession hold wands of willow topped with blue ribbons or with bunches of flowers. At certain points they make their inspection, and beat the boundary stones. But all these points are not easy to come at: through ware-

* See footnote to p. 84.

houses and private buildings they must seek them, and presently their journey brings them to the river's bank, where the southern boundary marches with the Thames. Here they take to the boats. And when all is done, there is still the new-minted shilling, earned, in this lenient age, at a very moderate expense.

WHITSUN

THE SEVENTH SUNDAY AFTER EASTER*

*He allowes of honest pastime, and thinks not the bones of the
dead any thing bruised, or the worse for it, though the Country
Lasses daunce in the church-yard after Evensong.*
SIR THOMAS OVERBERY—'*A Franklin*', 1615

IF Whitsun is now the phantom of its former self, the
explanation must be looked for in the character of its
gaiety, and that again was determined by the character, the
sacred meaning, of Pentecost. Of three events that chiefly
stabbed the year with joy, the Nativity, the Resurrection,
and the coming of the Holy Spirit, the third was the least
open to popular understanding. A birth in a stable can be
imagined, and clothed from early childhood in all the warm
and human symbolism of Christmas. Rebirth can be
imagined too, less easily perhaps, though on it is pinned the
most profound ambition of the human mind. But the gift
of Imagination itself is less imaginable. Instead of the inn at
Bethlehem and the garden at sunrise there is only that
unspecified "place" in which the Apostles were gathered
together, when "suddenly there came a sound from heaven
as of a rushing mighty wind, and it filled all the house where
they were sitting. And there appeared unto them cloven
tongues like as of fire, and it sat upon each of them. And
they were all filled with the Holy Ghost, and began to speak
with other tongues, as the Spirit gave them utterance".†

Christmas and Easter had their old foreshadowing in the
birth of the sun and the rebirth of the slain god; but pagan

* See Appendix A.
† *Acts*, II, 2–4.

[158]

theology could not foreshadow the event recorded in these words, or, with redeemed symbolism, nourish its memory. By the time flame-coloured Whitsun* arrived—seven weeks after Easter, and still too early for the solar bonfires of Midsummer that might well have become its property— Easter and May Day had together exhausted the best abundance of primeval Spring; yet not so completely but that Whitsun received the last spill of the cornucopia. Churches were filled with birch boughs breaking into leaf. But its pagan gaiety is gratuitous, married to the Christian feast by the mere exuberance of a Spring-time holiday, rather than by any true similarity of ideas. Nothing but joy, it seems, and the accident of time, has brought into conjunction the Whitsun Morris and the Feast of the tongues of fire.

In comparison with the two earlier festivals, English Whitsun was therefore weak in emblematic customs of a popular sort. An artificial dove might float to the altar on a wire, balls of fire and showers of rose leaves might descend in a few great churches, to the satisfaction of the congregation. But outside the church, in the towns and villages, Whitsun was really an extended holiday, a week of junketing, justified by Pentecost, but not representing it in symbols. The main feature of the holiday was the Whitsun Ale, a parish carousal derived from the Agapæ or love-feasts of the primitive Church, in those centuries when, as Aubrey puts it, "All the Congregation met and feasted, after they had received the Communion together; and those that were rich brought for themselves and the poor, and all eate together, for the encrease of mutuall love, and for the rich to shew their love and charity to the poor.

* Flame-coloured, yet the word is derived from "Hwíta Sunnandaeg", or "White Sunday", probably so named because large numbers were baptised at Pentecost, and the Saxon people were impressed by the sight of so many snow-white garments.

"In every parish was a church-house," he says—some of them are standing at this time—"to which belonged spits, crocks, and other utensils for dressing provisions. Here the housekeepers met. The young people were there too, and had dauncing, bowling, shooting at buttes, etc., the ancients sitting gravely by, and looking on."* The churchwardens were in command: it was they who laid in the malt, and provided the beer that would be sold at the banquet, and the profit given to the poor, "according to the Christian rule that all festivity should be rendered innocent by alms." They usually arranged for other entertainments of the kind, known simply as Church Ales, one of them on the Village Festival or Saint's day, but then the greater part of the takings might be entered against church expenses. At Christmas, charity was given, as a rule, individually: but at Whitsun, collectively: the Apostles had been gathered together "in unity of purpose",† and the sense of *communal* action was strong at this festival. The poor of the parish relied on it; and sometimes, to swell the fund, a tree or a garlanded Maypole was erected by the door of the church, and beneath it the girls of the village stationed themselves after service to beg an alms of the many emerging communicants. There would be many that day, for at Whitsun, of course, every man must make his communion.

But we must not draw too rosy a picture of ancestral virtue. Obedience and generosity were not always uppermost in their minds. In the churchyard, on the North side of the church, a "Robin Hood's Bower" had been built out of branches, garlands and ribbons; and here the rustic "Lord" and "Lady" of the Whitsun Ale were enthroned, with a Mace-Bearer and Fool to attend them. This arbour

* John Aubrey: *The Natural History of Wiltshire*, p. 33.
† Mgr. Knox's translation, 1945.

was directly descended from those that St. Augustine had
been told to approve, and it probably looked much the
same. It was in this part of the churchyard, where few were
buried, that the people had always danced away the long
Summer evenings, when the doors had been opened after
Evensong; and Whitsun was above all the time of the Morris.
For several weeks the young men who composed the local
team had devoted an evening or two to rehearsal, and their
leader had been in touch with the churchwardens. In the
wardens' accounts of the fifteenth, sixteenth and seventeenth centuries there are many entries that concern them.
Payment would be made for a hobby-horse, for dancing
bells and beer, and for the dancing itself. The Morris men
were held to be lawful entertainers—though not by all. Let
us see them through the unloving eyes of Philip Stubbes, as
they and their followers prepare to invade God's Acre on
the Sabbath evening.

"First, all the wilde-heds of the Parish, conventing
together, chuse them a Graund-Captain (of all mischeef)
whome they innoble with the title of 'my Lord of Mis-rule',
and him they crowne with great solemnitie, and adopt for
their king. This king anointed chuseth forth twentie, fortie,
threescore or a hundred lustie Guttes, like to him self, to
waighte upon his lordly Maiestie, and to guarde his noble
person. Then, everie one of these his men, he investeth
with his liveries of green, yellow, or some other light
wanton colour; And as though that were not (bawdie)
gawdie enough, I should say, they bedecke them selves with
scarfs, ribons & laces hanged all over with golde rings,
precious stones, & other iewels: this doon, they tye about
either leg xx or xl bels, with rich handkerchiefs in their
hands, and sometimes lay a crosse over their shoulders
& necks, borrowed for the most parte of their pretie

Mopsies & looving Bessies, for bussing them in the dark.

"Thus al things set in order, then have they their Hobby-horses, dragons & other Antiques, togither with their baudie Pipers and thundering Drummers to strike up the devils daunce withall. then, marche these heathen company towards the Church and the Church-yard, their pipers pipeing, their drummers thundring, their stumps dauncing, their bels iyngling, their handkerchefs swinging about their heds like madmen, their hobbie-horses and other monsters skirmishing amongst the rout; and in this sorte they go to the Church (I say) & into the Church (though the Minister be at praier or preaching), dancing & swinging their handker-chiefs over their heds in the Church, like devils incarnate, with such a confuse noise, that no man can hear his own voice. Then, the foolish people they looke, they stare, they laugh, they fleer, and mount upon fourmes and pews to see these goodly pageants solemnised in this sort. Then, after this, about the Church they goe again, and againe, & so foorth into the church-yard where they have commonly their Sommer-haules, their bowers, arbors and banqueting houses set up, wherein they feast, banquet & daunce at that day, & (peradventure) all the night too. And thus these terrestriall furies spend the Sabaoth day."*

Whether Stubbes had ever set eyes on the Morris dancers; whether they were truly so many and so marvellous; whether they were actually permitted, here and there in the sleep of the Church, to jig their way widdershins across a general confession, or only pictured in that minacious and fecund imagination—it is surely true that no words have ever danced after them with more nimble relish and irrepressible sympathy. We are inclined to apply to their author the judgement passed by Blake on Milton: "He

* Philip Stubbes, *Anatomie of Abuses*, 1583.

was a true Poet, and of the Devil's party without knowing it."

But Stubbes never questioned that mischievously equivocating manuscript. "Why should they," he insisted, at the sheer effrontery of such idleness, "why should they abstaine from bodely labor, peradventure the whole week, spending it in drunkennesse, whordome, gluttonie, and other filthie Sodomiticall exercyses?"

It is precisely the extended idleness, with all that it entailed of good and bad, that has been lopped off from our festivals. The domestic customs remain, but the leisure has gone; and with it most of the outdoor kinds of celebration, the dances, the fêtes and fairs. William Howitt attributed the popularity of Whitsun in the nineteenth century to the village habit of 'club walking', which took the place of the earlier Whitsun Ale.* There were men's clubs and women's clubs, and they would march about the lanes in their finery behind a band—top-hats rosetted and be-ribboned, a sash to every waist, and banners held aloft—to conclude the day happily, not in the church house for the benefit of the poor, but in a public house to the great advantage of the publican: the Agapæ certainly had a strange posterity. Now, in turn, club walking has largely† vanished, and Whitsun week, like Easter week, has contracted to a formless Bank Holiday. For Whitsun, as we have seen, is poor in domestic customs fitted to survive in the contemporary air. Remove the banqueting and dancing, the Whitsun Ale and the club festivity, and what remains, we may ask, but a dish of gooseberries: the Whitsun gooseberries that a few families remember to eat on this day?—And, of course, the car: the crowd on the by-pass, the fire on the common, the sandwich paper in the wood.

* *The Rural Life of England*, 1838. Part II, p. 182.
† If not entirely; though here and there it was still kept up with music in the 1930's.

But are we to conclude that the banqueting and dancing and walking are finally abandoned? Evidence would be brought by some to show that, in recent years, it is otherwise. They would instance the revival of the Morris in the Midlands—the children walking in white through certain towns in the North—the Springhead Festival of the 1930's—and all the gusto of the English Folk Dance Society, with its membership of twenty thousand and more, and its yearly meetings in the Albert Hall to perform the Sword Dance and the Morris.

It may be agreed that modern living is private to the point of selfishness. But whether it can be made more communal, at Whitsun, by an accurate return to the ancient forms of entertainment appears to be a question of the kind which schoolboys are taught to introduce, in Latin, with the adverb *num*. Consider one character common to both Morris and Sword Dance. Are Englishmen any longer delighted by a local comic who runs among them in odd stockings, wheezing "You lazy rascal!" and other hoary witticisms, to belabour them with a pig's bladder? Admittedly the antics of the Fool are mere embroidery to the measures of the dance, which may be as well executed as they ever have been. But it does seem that the Folk Dance Movement will need to escape from an atmosphere of whimsy, exuded by the very word "Folk", if it is ever to introduce the English dances into English life again. Children can walk in white and gyre about the Maypole naturally enough; but these were the dances of grown men, exhausting and not without dignity: the agility of the Women's Institute only renders the Morris ridiculous.

The writer is aware that recent attempts to revive, in a modified form, the love-feasts of the early Church have met with a degree of success. Communicants breakfast together, and there seems to be nothing antiquarian about it. But this book is not concerned with the benefits that might result if the habit became general. In any case the incentive to a less featureless Whitsun is likely to come from the Church, if it comes at all. The season was a great one for the 'Miracles' and 'Mysteries' of the Middle Ages, so popular at the time of Chaucer. Twenty-five guilds at Chester combined to present a fairly comprehensive drama, which opened with the Creation of the World and closed with the Last Judgement. But to describe it as one drama is somewhat misleading. Each guild undertook a particular scene, more or less independently of the others, and presented it in several parts of the town on a movable stage, a kind of high cart with a superstructure. Thus, the Drapers acted the Creation, the Tanners the Fall of Lucifer, and the Water Carriers the Flood.* Some of the old accounts have survived: —"Paid for setting the world on fire, 4d." A modern scientist would be lucky to receive as much.

The present-day enlistment of the arts in a sacred cause is not confined to the Christmas season. Flame-red tulips and geraniums on the altar point the symbol. The feast of the Spirit might be regarded in, a special way as the feast of the imagination, and therefore of the arts—in a society, of course, where the arts were in open alliance with the Spirit.

* A. R. Wright and T. E. Lones, *British Calendar Customs*, 1936–8, Vol. I.

MIDSUMMER DAY

JUNE 24TH

ST. JOHN THE BAPTIST

With some delightful ostentation, or show, or pageant, or antick,
or fire-work.

WILLIAM SHAKESPEARE—*Love's Labour Lost*

THE longest day between rise and set of the sun, the shortest shadows at noon—something of ancient magic clings still to the temporal antipodes of Christmas, and clings therefore to Midsummer Day, even though it coincides but roughly with the Summer Solstice. Stonehenge is the reminder of that solar magic in all its potency: a ruin nearly twice as old as Christianity, and destined perhaps to outlast any building in Britain. Compared with its elemental solidity, time-battered but obstinate in the waste of Salisbury Plain, St. Paul's dome is the merest egg-shell.

Because the green roads of the hilltops converge on this point from all directions, and from parts of England as remote as the Mendips and East Anglia, Stonehenge appears to have been the hub of Iberian Britain. Here in this century the crowds arrive by car and bicycle, at dawn on the twenty-first, to see the sun rise over the "Friars' Heel", and to imagine, that instant, the knife descending on the victim which popular anthropology has provided for them. But the solar cult, of which Stonehenge and Avebury are the outstanding monuments, left also long-lasting memorials in human behaviour.* On Midsummer Eve large bonfires were

* See Sir James Frazer, *The Golden Bough*, Pt. IV, Bk. 1, Chap. X, "The Gardens of Adonis"; William Hone, *The Every-Day Book*, cols. 845–855, illustration, col. 823; Bourne, and Brand, works already mentioned, Midsummer chapters.

constructed, and at midnight they were lit. It is said that not many centuries ago a dozen could be seen at a time, blazing in the villages, and round them there were figures moving in rhythm, young men and garlanded girls, dancing and tossing violets and verbena into the flames. And then as the glow dwindled and the northern horizon, which had never throughout the night been wholly obscured, began to quicken again, but now farther to the East, the men were seizing the girls and vaulting them over the embers for good luck, or else they were driving the cattle through with pitchforks, and finally they were all pulling out lighted brands and running wild about the low houses of the village, huddled together as if in opposition to the atavistic sunrise. But somewhere a rotten cartwheel had been carried to a hilltop, bound with straw and tow, and with a stake through its nave to guide it; and at midnight, bursting into flame, it had gone rolling down into the valley,

> Resembling much the sunne that from the Heavens
> down should fal,
> A strange and monstrous sight it seemes, and
> fearefull to them all.*

If it had reached the valley still burning, to be quenched in river or pond, Destiny would smile.

The atmosphere of that night was indeed thick with magic, Oberon's magic. If a girl walked backward into the garden, uttered no word, but picked a rose and put it away unseen until Christmas, it would be found as crisp and fragrant that morning as the night she picked it, and her future husband would come up to her and take it out of her dress. But charms and divinations are not the theme of this

* Barnabe Googe, *The Popish Kingdome*, 1570, Bk. 4.

book. Enough to say that this dying Festival of Fire persisted even into the last century, and still betrayed in its keeping, however varied from district to district, the worship of the sun.

But all that is conveyed of rapture in the words "High Summer", and all the dreamlike enchantment bequeathed to that night by a single Shakespeare play must not deceive us. It was not rapture that inspired the observances of midnight, but apprehension. Midsummer was the festival of an archaic and dimly-remembered dread. On that day Autumn appeared on the skyline. Thereafter, warmth and light would diminish, the sun would fall from heaven, and with the ageing of the God would approach all the dangers and privations of the cold. By the same paradox, the first festival of hope in the year was Midwinter with its Spring-ward look. Thus at Midsummer the withdrawing sun must be propitiated with sacrifice and enheartened with imitative fire; and if only one drop of his potency could be preserved in a single rose until Christmas, the continuance of warmth would surely be vouchsafed.

Less obvious would be the association of *water* with Midsummer if we did not remember that men saw in the sun the fountainhead of all fertility. In the words of Akhenaten's *Hymn to the Sun*, "Thou placest a Nile in Heaven that it may rain upon us." But the lofty religion of Tel el Amarna was both brief and unique. It would be more to the point to mention the god Tammuz of Babylon and Carthage, whose name is thought to have signified "True son of the deep water", and whose image was bathed in water at the Summer Solstice. Indeed there were Midsummer rites involving the use of water throughout the ancient world. Sacred rivers and springs and the sea itself acquired, that night, strange properties of blessing and healing, and in many lands there were men and women bathing themselves and washing in the dew at the instant of sunrise.

Midsummer fires were condemned outright by the early Fathers. The ruling was in force with all Christians, but was specially intended, as Brand says, "to deter *Clergy-men* from this superstitious instance of Agility". For even the "Cloth" had been known to foot it in honour of the sun. And still, in this island, all of eighteen hundred years were required to see an end of those capers! But in handling the idolatry of water the Church had adopted the other and wiser policy. Baptism was itself baptised. Fortunately a Saint existed in whose name it could be done very happily. Midsummer Day became the Feast of St. John the Baptist, and all the supernatural amenities of that night and sunrise were thereafter attributed to this blunt and humble man. At Laughton in Yorkshire the Midsummer Fair was held in the churchyard. The church stands high on a hill, and the patron saint is St. John. It even became accepted that the fires were kindled in his honour. "But," as Bourne justly observes, "if this was Reason formerly, as it's probable it was (it having been a common thing, to shadow out Times and Seasons by Emblems) yet the Custom was originally instituted upon another Bottom."

Rising before sunrise to wash in the dew is not yet everywhere fallen into disuse, and might be remembered where there are children, for the reason that recommends it on May Day: the superstition evaporated, the delight remains. Certainly this hinge of time and apex of the natural year should be marked for them in some manner, or it will come and go unnoticed and unenjoyed. It is not unnoticed in the Lake District, where, even in the years of war, the delightful ceremony of Rushbearing has been kept up.*

* Not everywhere at Midsummer, however.

Rushes were formerly the only carpets in both house and church, and here they are still bringing them to church, worked into elaborate patterns, with many curious devices, a floral harp, it may be, or the infant Moses discovered in his bulrush cradle.* There exists no evening as suitable as the Eve for a performance of *A Midsummer Night's Dream* in a setting half natural and half formal, like the templed gardens of Stowe or the clipped yews of Compton Winyates; and this calls to mind some words from that Elizabethan Survey of London already mentioned. "On the Vigil of St. John Baptist, every Man's Door being shadowed with green Birch, Long Fennel, St. John's Wort, Orpin, White Lillies, and such like, garnished upon with Garlands of beautiful Flowers, had also Lamps of Glass, with Oil burning in them all the Night: Some hung out Branches of Iron, curiously wrought, containing Hundreds of Lamps lighted at once." Such lights are obsolete except, it may be, at a performance of the "Dream", or at a Midsummer ball, but in any event our rooms may be filled with a profusion of June flowers and herbs. That witty and well-beloved man, the Vicar of Morwenstow, in whom worship and pleasure were not to be disunited, would fill his church on the Cornish cliff with roses and southernwood for a Midsummer service,† and then lead out his whole congregation to the village green, for the dancing and wrestling and running that he himself had initiated.

The Midsummer bonfires are out, and are unlikely to be relit. Ritual flames are reserved for Guy Fawkes in the present century. But there exists a kind of ceremonial fire which has immensely grown in popularity, even while the more ancient kind was decaying. Fireworks‡ have, for us,

---

* Christina Hole, *English Custom and Usage*, 1941.
† S. Baring-Gould, *The Vicar of Morwenstow*, 1876, p. 61.
‡ See A. St. H. Brock, *Pyrotechnics*, 1922, also his *Fêtes and Fireworks*, 1946 (a Puffin book); article in *Enc. Brit.*; and *Fireworks and How to Make Them*, 1871 (a Routledge Handbook)—for the passages quoted in this chapter.

no sacred meaning, whether pagan or Christian, and they do not belong to any one day of the year. But they have their season. Winter nights are mostly too cold for their enjoyment; nor do they need inky darkness for background. They are perhaps never so lovely as when they begin; in a warm, late twilight, before the birds have fallen silent; when woods and water are still visible; and while there remains enough strength in the sky to weaken the first mottling of chance stars that are put into it. To Summer they belong, and therefore to Midsummer. Probably the earliest annual display in Europe was that given in Florence on this evening, the Eve of St. John; for we may be sure that it was at no time introduced as a novelty, but gradually flowered out of the pagan torches and bonfires we have already described. Thus both history and the season seem to point to this night for a festival of fire such as the builders of Stonehenge would stand agape at.

Pyrotechny, Art of Fire, comes to us out of the Ancient East. China or India gave it birth, and at a date so remote that we cannot even hazard a guess at it; nor has the East relinquished the art. Travellers, fortunate enough to see them, speak of the mysterious charm of Chinese displays; and of the Japanese delight in symmetry—for there the stars break, not over-brilliant, but with the precision of Euclid.

Yet the East, if we exclude Japan, has been slow to develop the technique. It is to the chemists and Firemasters of Europe, and above all of England, that we owe our modern virtuousity.

"Greek Fire" and other fiery weapons are almost cœval with war itself, and in Ancient Rome fire seems to have been used in some way for entertainment. Yet the earliest true *displays* in Europe are probably those of the sixteenth century. At the Chester Races of 1610, held on St. George's

Day, there appeared "Two men in green ivy, with black hair and black beards, very ugly to behold, and garlands upon their heads, with great clubs in their hands, with fireworks to scatter abroad". Here, clearly, is the Green Man of the old Spring ritual, whom we have already encountered on May Day. But it is interesting to find him equipped with these novel toys—still rather novel in England—with rocket and cracker and "fire-club", this last a primitive Roman Candle brandished on the top of a staff. We associate his leafiness rather with water than with fire. Yet, as we have seen, fire and water, emblems of sunlight and rain, had long been used together in the promotion of growth.*

But it was in Baroque Italy, and from the marriage of fire with architecture, that the art developed. A wooden palace would be built on the Piazza, with the utmost elaboration of ornament, and over and around and within this structure the fire must play, accentuating column and cornice, glowing within splendid "transparencies", leaping in flame from the mouths and eyes of statues. Hardly less lavish were the displays in contemporary England. And with us a favourite site was the centre of the Thames opposite Whitehall. Between the crowning of James II and the Peace Celebrations of 1946 many indeed must have been the festive stars repeated in that long mirror.

But national occasions apart, the eighteenth-century Englishman—or at least the eighteenth-century Londoner—had good opportunities for indulging his delight in fireworks. For presently all the fashionable Pleasure Gardens were competing in this field, and by then we no longer depended on the skill of the foreign Firemaster. Exactly how good were these entertainment technically? Let us try to see

---

* As was mentioned on p. 150, the Green Man was a feature of the *chimney-sweepers'* May Day.

them through the eyes of a contemporary.   When Charles
Lamb was describing to Wordsworth the Peace Celebrations
of 1814, he wrote of rockets "floundering about in space
like unbroke horses", and of "the still finer showers of gloomy
rain that fell sulkily and angrily from 'em".   The words are
surely suggestive.   A modern writer would hardly choose
them to describe the opening of "Golden Rain" or "Demon
Flash".   To modern eyes, we think, the demons of that
night would appear a little drowsy, the gilding of those
showers a little tarnished.   But indeed we are sure of it.
True colour was impossible until the introduction of
potassium chlorate about this time, and true brilliance, the
bemusing brilliance of modern fireworks, came only with
magnesium and aluminium, much later in the century.

Then fire was divorced from architecture.   At the end of
the Crimean war a display was given that was entirely
worked in fire, and all subsequent displays have been of this
kind, including of course the great series at the Crystal
Palace, begun in 1865 and lasting to within recent memory.
It was notably here that England proved her leadership in the
art.   And yet we may see in this modern development not
so much an artistic as a technical advance; and if we judge
them as works of art, rather than as breath-taking spectacles,
we may wonder if the earlier displays were not finer
achievements, for all the faintness of their colours and the
fewness of their effects.   But the comparison is difficult.
Perhaps we should say, rather, that the possibilities of delight
were never so ample in a former age, and are far from fully
explored in our own.

Fireworks are among the purest expressions of joy that
are possible to man.   Supremely useless, like singing and
dancing, they are even briefer than a song or a figure, and by
their brevity move us the more.   They have no flavour of

eternity, like music and certain buildings; for they are this world's joy, haunted and sharpened by impermanence. And they shock us. They startle our dullness, and release us from our caution. If it is true that we cannot look long at an upward fountain without finding in it, however remotely, the idea of aspiration; then here it is even more aspiration, with elation, elevation of heart, that we derive from these gestures in a darkening sky. Listen to their names:

> Golden and Silver Rains and Showers and Fountains,
> Brilliant Suns and Stars, and Huge Revolving Suns,
> Rainbow Candles, Rainbow Wheels and Showers,
> Glittering Cascades, Glorias and Brilliant Yew Trees.

They speak of the April weather, the storms and rejoicing of that mythical landscape—heavenly it may be, after all, though earthly in transience, for its forms are those of the earth translated.

While we watch, we do not care about names, and rightly. Yet a name has something to add to enjoyment. Many are now traditional, others of recent invention, and most of them mentioned here are used by Brock, the world-famous English firm whose 'Benefits' have passed into the language. Still, when all is said of them, names are only trade-names; but the principal *types* of firework are permanent—Rocket and Gerb and Roman Candle—and also wholly distinct. It is from these that any display must be built up. A brief account of each type may therefore be found useful.

Shells

The most spectacular of fireworks. They are not rocket-propelled but are fired from the ground, and therefore they have no raging tail as they rise. Combinations of shape and colour and sound seem infinite. Perhaps the initial explosion may be followed by rapid fire, and the peppering of darkness with Rockets or squirming Tourbillons. Or a constellation of green and crimson stars with tails of contrasting colours— a new Ariadne's Crown—may break from the sky with a report, and descend slowly on pale threads in the shape of a dome or chandelier, with a tight clot of smoke at the apex, and a curiously insidious whispering.

Rockets

When ignited, a downward rage of sparks and fire instantly gushes from the base with a hollow roar, like the tongue of a prodigious blowlamp, and after a moment this is rushed up into the sky, sometimes with a loud surprising whistle that weakens away toward the star-shaking report. But from afar they are gentler and more compelling. We shall remember how the Rockets rose above the Thames in 1946 when all else in those two hours before midnight has been reduced to a vague impression of brightness. Ten—twenty—at a time, in gradual "bouquets", they lean up into the darkness, slide to the crown of flight, and there push onward a little farther, each one, a narrow spray of stars, till a cloud is formed, through which still further sprays are opening. No other firework holds the attention so well, or is the fruit of such careful hand-craftsmanship; and yet the Rocket is at least seven hundred years old and possibly older, and has changed remarkably little during that time.

The structure of the narrow case is twofold: the driving fire must eat its way—but only at the last moment, near the peak of the parabola—into the cap, stuffed full of "pumped stars" or "pinched stars", according to the method employed. Indeed, even the manufacture of fireworks is to the layman evocative of mystery. Nitrate of Strontia, Chlorate of

Baryta, Blue Calomel and Orpiment, Lampblack and Sugar of Milk, White Arsenic and Black Antimony—such are a few of the ingredients employed, familiar· enough to the chemist, but strange to the layman, to whom some of them might equally well signify ancient dishes or wild flowers. And when he reads that "after making, the stars are dried in specially constructed buildings", he feels that he has stumbled upon some gloss on the first chapter of Genesis.

Rockets open like Shells with quite as lovely effects of pattern and colour, if less tremendously. In a private display mere magnitude is no benefit, and it is better to lay out money on a good number of Rockets than on one or two expensive Shells or a Set Piece. Like the Shells in public displays, the larger Rockets are often harnessed together and launched simultaneously in "flights" or "bouquets", one after the other.

Mines

All their energy is expended in the wit and bravado of one utterance: the image, we may think it, of a sheaf of corn with dripping ears, one or two hundred feet in height, or of a golden cypress. But there are mines which include the functions of other fireworks. Thus the "Jack-in-the-Box" and the "Mine of Serpents" open like a Gerb or Fountain, but then, as a seventeenth-century writer expresses it, "after a pretty distance of time you shall heare a sudden noise and see all those fisgigs flying some one way, some another. This toy has given great content to the spectators."

Roman Candles

These are more modest than any of the fireworks described so far, but of a singular charm. When lit, they continue to burn for some time—hence "Candle"—throwing out eight or ten bright-coloured velvet stars in fairly quick succession.

NOCTURNAL FESTIVAL.
By Robin Jaques.

They are a mild firework; there is no initial report; the soft, lambent balls or stars are tossed up one after another in gentle expectoration. The fountain effect is increased when several are fixed at angles to a criss-cross lattice-work frame, to form a Jet, so that a whole "Bouquet" blossoms at once.

And yet these loveliest of Candles are not of Rome. They were, we have excellent reason to believe, invented in England. The same seventeenth-century writer describes them as "a trunck of fire which shall cast forth divers fire-balls". But at first they were carried about on a club, such as the Green Man waved on his way to the Chester Races.

Gerbs and Fountains

The name Gerb is derived from '*gerbe*', the French for a cornsheaf, and signified in England a fountain of water before it was applied to a fountain of fire. Lit on the ground, it burns for a minute or two, casting up into the air the shape of a glittering, legendary tree, from the crown of which there continually falls on every side, with a loud or soft persistent roar, a curiously slow shower of twitching golden leaves and blossoms, or clouds of golden pollen; and these, striking the ground, continue, it appears, to bounce and tumble about at the foot of the tree, so that the ground is all the while crawling with light, while smoke drifts away in billows at the top, or can be seen trickling downward in the most delicate of wisps. Gerbs are gold, and Fountains silver; the one type louder, fiercer and higher; the other more moderate, and seemingly slow. But the "Mystic Tree" and the "Brilliant Yew Tree"—both of them apparently weeping trees—are composed of many Fountains in diminishing tiers, which not only open into colour, but are apt to change their colour—red, violet, orange, green—throughout a remarkable, short season.

Wheels and Tourbillons

From the humblest Catherine to the noblest of Revolving Suns there are many varieties of Wheel. One spasm of energy, and they are off at high speed, with much rhythmical fuss and confusion. Sometimes they appear to hesitate in mid-course, change gear and colour simultaneously, and accelerate away, flinging their fume of sparks still wider and wider. Sometimes they spin in both directions at once, with rainbows of colour in the centre and strange intersecting circles of fire. Then there are horizontal Wheels, designed, of course, to throw their finery upward; and others that are neither horizontal nor vertical, but both, and more besides, for they illustrate extension in more planes than we can count or follow. The "Grand Volute" of the last century is a fine extension of this idea. Above the wheel rises a diminishing spiral frame, its point fixed to the vertical axis. Wheel and spiral are covered with fireworks which cause it to revolve at great speed, so that a screw of fire appears to be continually twisting up into nothing. As for Tourbillons, they are not fastened to a frame or post but are laid flat on the ground. There they revolve so fast in a froth of golden sparks that suddenly they are lifted noisily into the air, till, at the height of about fifty or perhaps a hundred feet, they scribble themselves into silence.

Waterfalls

The fireworks hang vertically from a rope between upright poles. When they are lit all at once, a solid curtain of dazzling white sparks begins to be let down, with a soft noise like tearing material, and leaps and froths at the foot of the fall, while a cloud of milky white smoke billows away from the crest. Although quite effective when only two poles are used with eight or ten cases between them, this

"Niagara" can be extended to great width—to the width of a Thames bridge, for example. The "Weird White Waterfall" of the Crystal Palace was sometimes ninety feet high and several hundred feet long.

Water Fireworks

The old Firemasters were not slow to exploit the beauties of reflection. They liked to give their displays from barges anchored mid-stream, or from the opposite bank to the audience; and we are wise to follow their example whenever we can. But they also designed fireworks that would explode on the surface of the water. For the most part these did not differ from ordinary fireworks except that they were fitted with floats. Bright, deciduous trees blossoming—to all appearances—upwards and downwards at once, and with their golden or silver petals falling and rising simultaneously, to vanish at the point of contact—this loveliness can be imagined, and is worth contriving.

Fire and water may be still more intimate: there are fireworks designed to make them so. One is the Skimmer Rocket, a Rocket that is fired without stick or final explosion, and horizontally. As the name implies, it skims over the water, bouncing and sometimes plunging beneath it, on an unpredictable course. Another is a kind of coughing Gerb which utters continuously, but with spasms of additional zest, from which recoiling, it is momentarily driven beneath the surface, to emerge still voluble.

Portraits and Pictures

Tolerable likenesses of the King and Queen, or of some distinguished foreigner with collar and tie and spectacles, appear on the skyline, looking this way and that, in the set-piece that so often concludes a large display. This kind of piece is known as Lancework, and consists of a high lattice-work frame to which the designs are fastened. On one occasion a big bunch of primroses appeared—faded—and was suddenly Lord Beaconsfield himself. Occasionally the designs are comic by intention.

LAMMAS

THE FIRST SUNDAY IN AUGUST

ANCIENTLY AUGUST 1ST

Thou shalt eat the labours of thy hands: O well is thee, and
happy shalt thou be.

Psalm CXXVII, 2

OF the four agricultural festivals—Plough Sunday and
Monday, Rogationtide, Lammas, and the Harvest—Lammas
alone is without secular customs, a purely sacred occasion.
No festival in the particular sense intended by the present
writer, it yet demands inclusion in this book, for to speak
of three is to imply the fourth; without it the cycle of
growth would be incomplete, and it happens that its place
in the cycle has been recently remembered.

According to the Oxford Dictionary, the name is derived
from the Anglo-Saxon "hláfmaesse"—or in the modern
equivalent "loaf-mass"—"a festival at which loaves of bread
were consecrated, made from the first ripe corn"; and this
derivation is no longer in serious doubt. In the Middle Ages
the harvest itself, the in-gathering, remained virtually a
heathen festival, its primitive uses very lightly disguised or
corrected. Thomas Hardy would have us believe that even
in the nineteenth century the countryman, or at any rate
the country woman, remained a pagan at heart. "Women,"
he says, "whose chief companions are the forms and faces
of outdoor Nature retain in their souls far more of the Pagan

[181]

G

fantasy of their remote forefathers than of the systematised religion taught their race at a later date." Archaic joys of the Harvest Home will be described in the following chapter. Nothing like the modern Harvest Thanksgiving seems to have existed in mediæval times: the Christian event of the season was Lammas, the first communion in the bread of the new corn, though this too may well have replaced some earlier ritual. Lammas appears to have been a specially Anglo-Saxon occasion. It may have slowly declined in Norman England; it may have been moribund a long while before the Reformation; certain it is that at the Reformation it vanished, along with many another symbolic and beautiful practice, supposed at that time, not without justification, to have become an idolatry.

Now, after a lapse of four or five centuries—the old objection no longer relevant—the Church of England begins to remember the festival of first fruits. Already a number of parishes keep Lammas on the first Sunday in August, especially in the South of England, and the custom is spreading. Mr. Andrew Young, the poet, has written a finely worded hymn for the occasion, 'Lord, by whose breath all souls and seeds are living,' and this has been put to music, and will shortly be published in the B.B.C. hymn book.

A few sentences from *The Plough*, the periodical of the West Sussex Church and Countryside Association, will reveal the ideas that underlie the present revival.* "The purpose of the Lammas Service is to offer the first of the crops to God: and to offer Him the first food made in the village from these early crops. It is not so much a thanksgiving, though obviously that element must be included. It is an offering, irrespective of what the results have been, or are to be. A sheaf

* *The Plough*, Lammastide, 1945.

of corn, and a loaf (made from the wheat that has just ripened) are brought to church by members of the village and farming communities." Generally a farm labourer offers the sheaf, and a baker the loaf, and members of the Young Farmers' Club take other parts in the service. Occasionally the service begins in a field, where the sheaf is cut, and afterwards taken to the church porch and then to the altar. The form varies a little from parish to parish. To conclude with another sentence from *The Plough*—"The next logical stage is for the bread to be used at the Holy Communion; only a few parishes have reached this stage as yet, though it must always have been an integral part of the ancient service."

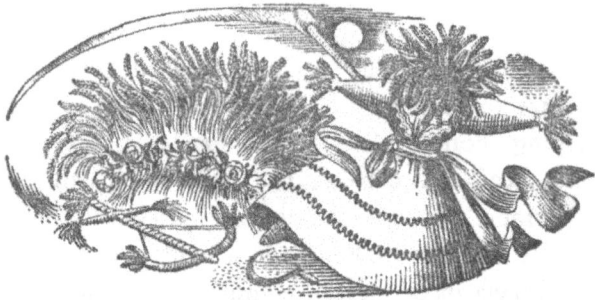

THE HARVEST

For the shouting for thy summer fruits and for thy harvest is fallen. And gladness is taken away, and joy out of the plentiful field.

Isaiah XVI, 9

THE women are clustering to watch, and in the field there is an air of excitement and pleasure, for the reapers have worked their way to the centre, and the last ears have gone down. As they fell they were caught up by the oldest of the harvesters, and now he is rapidly twisting and weaving them into a curious device. Between his hands it is beginning to assume the likeness of a little man—a harvest manikin, bound at waist and neck with bright-coloured ribbon, with bristling_ head, and stark arms outstretched. While he works the reapers are forming a circle about him. Now he plants his feet apart, grips the manikin firmly with both hands, and slowly lowers it to the ground, and as he does so, the others imitate him. Hats and caps are twitched off, backs bent, and a circle of fingers touches the stubble. Then all at once the company break into a long-drawn, musical cry. What they are saying is simply, "The Neck!" But the words are stretched out so as to continue all the while the men are raising themselves very slowly into an upright position, and then lifting their hats above their heads. And in the middle the corn manikin has been exalted too. This they do three times, and then three times again, but now with different words—"The Neck! The Neck! The Neck!" they cry—"We have 'un! We have 'un! We have 'un!" Then at the last elevation they all burst into loud and delighted laughter, fling hats and caps in the air, caper about and begin kissing the girls. But one young man has snatched the "Neck" after a scuffle, and is now running at top speed towards the farm. At the door a milkmaid is standing with a pail of water. The sound of the chanting has reached her across the fields, and she is listening for the runner's footsteps. She will souse him if she can, but if he is clever enough to enter the house unwetted, still carrying the puppet, she must yield him a kiss.

This Devon custom of "Crying the Neck" was kept up well into the last century, and in other parts of England something very similar might be seen.—It is just possible that a few old countrymen still remember it. A gentleman farmer, writing for Hone's *Every-Day Book* in 1826, tells us that "on a fine still autumn evening" it had "a wonderful effect at a distance. I have once or twice heard upwards of twenty men cry it, and sometimes joined by an equal number of female voices. About three years back, on some high grounds where our young people were harvesting, I heard six or seven 'necks' cried in one night, although I know that some of them were four miles off. They are heard throughout the quiet evening air, at a considerable distance sometimes. But I think that the practice is beginning to decline of late, and many farmers and their men do not care about keeping up this old custom. I shall always patronise it myself, because I take it in the light of a thanksgiving."

The writer did not know how ancient a ritual he described. Centuries before Christ, Greek travellers in Egypt and Asia

Minor were intrigued to observe the reapers huddled together, lifting hands and voices in a long melancholy and repetitive cry. Herodotus was one who thought it worthy of note, but he missed the explanation provided in modern times by the anthropologist. Enlightened now, we may say that the reapers of Devon were still lamenting, beside the new railway to Exeter, the death of Osiris, the Corn Spirit, mortally wounded by their sickles, driven back into the last ears, and there finally murdered—lamenting his needful death, and imploring by ritual observance his continued blessing and forgiveness.

To propitiate the Spirit of the Harvest by murdering a man was still the practice of many primitive peoples in the last century, and once it may have been universal. The Bible records it (II Samuel, 21): our own Teutonic ancestors perhaps did the same. The victim died 'for' the God in two senses, both as sacrifice and representative, and he was often treated with reverence before his execution. We may see in the holder of the sacred "Neck" the spiritual descendant of that victim, who in some parts of England was still roughly handled after a thousand years of Christianity; while to souse him with water has been interpreted as an act of imitative magic, a charm to bring plentiful rain on the seed of the new year.

With these implications never wholly expunged from that abyss of memory where the archaic images survive, it is not surprising that there was some reluctance to cut those final haunted ears in which the wild Spirit had taken refuge. In South Wales and in the Midlands they used to tie them into a bunch and then throw at it with hatchets from a distance, as if to distribute the responsibility. In some counties it must have been thought that the Spirit withdrew, before the rhythmical advance of the reapers, from one farm to another, and took refuge and was finally executed in the last field of the most backward husbandman. For in modern times when a farmer finished before his neighbour there was much amusement in the field. Immediately a labourer sprang on the cart to shout the guilt-shifting formula amid applause. "This be tu give notice that Mr. Pickard has ge'un the hook a turn and sent th' owd Hare into Mr. Easterbrook's standen corn!" A country God might well assume the body of that wild and fleetfoot creature. He was thought to do so at Easter. And now for a moment the God became visible again, bolting from the protection of the dwindling corn.

But the horror of blood had long since evaporated from the Saxon harvest-fields, even before the barbarians invaded, leaving only a nameless apprehension—and that by no means ubiquitous—to put a fine edge on the rejoicing. And how much a festival of joy was this, with its earthly flavour of accomplishment, unique among the festivals of promise! Twelfth Night, Plough Monday, Holy Thursday, Midsummer, Lammas—they all speak of the Harvest. The Harvest speaks only of itself, or of the Hand of Providence. "They joy before Thee according to the joy in harvest," said Isaiah. Between the "Crying of the Neck" and the lifting of the corn there had been days of anxiety, but now the last load is about to be taken in, and there will be no serious work on the farm for a week. It is the hour of the Harvest Home.

Already the waggon has been drawn into the field behind a team of horses. There are garlands to their necks and ears, and sunflowers and scarlet ribbons to their blinkers. The captain of the reapers, crowned with flowers himself, directs the loading, and as soon as the last sheaf is lifted the children of the farm scramble on top, with the branches and festoons they have been preparing for this moment. On the leading horse is seated—surely in allusion to some half-remembered provincial Ceres?—the prettiest girl of the farm, dressed in white, with corn and flowers in her straw bonnet and a yellow sash to her waist. And high over all is raised up emblematically the "Ivy Girl" or "Corn Baby": a single sheaf from the best corn in the field, sometimes "made into a human shape; curiously dressed by the women, and adorned with paper trimmings, cut to resemble a cap, ruffles, handkerchief, etc., of the finest lace".* Occasionally the load may support a life-sized figurehead. "I have seen," says Hutchinson in his *History of Northumberland*, "in some places, an image apparelled in great finery, crowned with flowers, a sheaf of corn placed under her arm, and a sickle in her hand, carried out of the village in the morning of the conclusive reaping day, with music and much clamour of the reapers, into the field, where it stands fixed on a pole all day, and when the reaping is done, is brought home in like manner. This they call the harvest queen." But their Nordic ancestors in Germany would have said that it represented the primordial monarch called "Sheaf".†

And so the harvest came home, attended by all who had been at work in the fields, with flags and ribbons from the top, with pipe and drum beneath, and with songs and laughter. "It is donne with great joy and merriment," says Aubrey, "and a Fidler rides on the loaded Cart, or Wayne, playing." In the farmyard the mistress and her daughters and maids, busy all day about the evening's banquet, were out to see it arrive, and as the symbolic load came to a standstill, as likely as not a young man leapt on the shafts, to bawl—

* William Hone, *The Every-Day Book*, Vol. 2, 1827, col. 1162.
† H. M. Chadwick, *The Origin of the English Nation*, 1907, Chap. XII.

THE HARVEST

"We have ploughed, we have sowed,
We have reaped, we have mowed,
We have brought home every load,
Hip, hip, hip, Harvest Home!"—

and the last two words would be shouted by everyone.
Then cake and beer were handed round by the girls, the load
was driven away to the stackyard, the team unharnessed and
put in the stable, and the men washed and spruced themselves up in new shirts and shiny boots for the supper. But
first the Corn Baby was taken into the house, where it
might remain for three or four years until its virtue was no
longer remembered.   In a few hours the harvest
moon would be buoyant on the skyline, a prodigious gourd.

"Thou shalt observe the feast of tabernacles seven days,
after that thou hast gathered in thy corn and thy wine: And
thou shalt rejoice in thy feast, thou, and thy son, and thy
daughter, and thy manservant, and thy maidservant, and the
Levite, the stranger, and the fatherless, and the widow, that
are within they gates   because the Lord thy God shall
bless thee in all thine increase, and in all the works of thine
hands, therefore thou shalt surely rejoice." So Moses ordered
in Deuteronomy XVI, and so it was still done in the England
of George IV. Under the protection of the new Corn Baby,
propped in a corner with muslin arms outstretched, or
revolving softly from the ceiling with its one archaic gesture
of fruitfulness, the whole company sat down to supper on
equal terms, distinction of class forgotten, master beside
man and "the stranger within the gates"; for farmers generally
helped one another to bring in the corn, as they do to this
day, and the visiting labourers were treated like those of the
house. There was roast beef and plum-pudding and a limit-
less flow of beer or cider. Presently they were all on their

[189]   G*

feet again toasting the farmer's wife in a sing-song catch, then the farmer himself, then his daughters—someone altering the words on the spur of the moment—then the plough, the sickle and the flails; and if anyone at this stage was too fuddled to remember the trick of the rhyme, the proper forfeit was imposed: he must drink again. At some time in the evening the farmer would distribute gifts to all his helpers: money or tobacco to the men; lace, ribbons and rows of pins to the girls. And there would be singing of the harvest songs, interrupted by brief bellows of chorus; old favourites called for; old voices, one after another, rasping away through interminable ballads, relishing the ancient crudities that never failed to enchant the men or to embarrass the young women.

Except for the not unfriendly stutter of a distant tractor, there is silence over the stubble-fields. Abundance is visible; "the moon," in Mr. Auden's words, "is usual"; and they are bringing in the last load of all—but there will be no one to welcome it in the yard. It comes in like any other consignment from the soil of England, that roofless food-factory, and the employees who walk behind it do not expect a week's holiday, or even a banquet with the manager. It certainly has come to pass in our island that "gladness is taken away, and joy out of the plentiful field".

Yet who will convince the up-to-date countryman that he has lost anything at all, duped as he is by the notion of infallible Progress? The delusion is carefully fostered by the newspapers, most of all when they speak with feigned regret of the quaintness of "the quaint old days". Songless and joyless in his work he may be, and cut off from spiritual union with his fellows and with the earth—but the Grid is coming to the village, and in the new cottages there will be "H. & C.".

Who will convince him that an attempt to restore that union is not the same thing as antiquarian sentimentality, for which he would reasonably claim that he has "no time"? "Man shall not live by bread alone." We do. And we find that, made without art or love, the bread itself becomes tasteless.

It is said that most farm labourers in the eighteenth century would not have worked for a master who failed to provide them with supper and song in the hour of achievement. At the next Candlemas Fair they would have engaged themselves to another farmer, and entered his service on the following Lady Day. Such men preserved the dignity of the Common People and had not acquired the outlook of wage-slaves. But we must be careful not to exaggerate. There are still farms in which a true sense of fellowship survives, and a smaller number in which it finds expression in some sort of harvest meal, though generally without much merriment. There may even be one or two in which the old Gods look for crumbs of comfort under strange names; though to know *that* would be merely amusing. At the beginning of the century a traveller in the North discovered a corn puppet, or "Kern Baby", placed in a wheatfield to keep away storms. The farmer's wife explained that prayers to God were all right, but "We mustn't forget owd Providence. Happen it's best to keep in wi' *both* parties".

Of the ancient structure of good sense and superstition and faith, only fragments remain. We need to replace it with a structure suited to our own age. "Crying the Neck," for example, is obsolete and quite unfitted for revival, in spite of its symbolic value. But the last corn to be lifted will always remain the emblem of completion, and this moment is one of those in the year which ought to be emphasised, if only in the awareness of a country childhood. "To the

Husbandman," wrote John Brand, "whom the Fear of Wet, Blights, etc., had harassed with great Anxiety, the Completion of his Wishes could not fail of imparting an enviable Gust of Delight." Children are naturally fond of ceremony, and with a little encouragement they would make of the last load an event nearly as festive as that already described.

But here is an actual Harvest Home of the 1930's, recorded by Mr. Rolf Gardiner in his book, *England Herself.* It is one of many, not at all designed for the enjoyment of children only. "A great procession would be formed of carts and waggons, and these decorated with boughs and garlands, the horses with dahlias in their bridles, and the workers of the estate in the waggons, the sixty campers on foot. All would sally forth to the field where the last stook of corn remained, and there the sheaves would be tossed up and then borne to Springhead and the church. Everyone joined in the service, and the camp might contribute a chorale. Afterwards campers, workers, their wives and guests would ascend the hill for the Harvest supper in the decorated barn. A flower-decked garland of corn hung from the lintel of the great doors, and within, corn-sheaves and flowers made festive that glowing hall of brick and flint, fire and candlelight." Good food, speeches and songs came after.

This is elaborate, but the harvest supper is so good an institution in any form that one cannot help thinking it will survive, and would even recover in a happier countryside. Two misfortunes caused it to decline: the decay of farming, and the decay of mutual respect between master and man. Clearly, without prosperity one cannot hope for a richer habit of living. 'Master and man' will remain as long as humans collaborate; but in theory the Harvest Home could be kept as happily in a 'Collective Farm' as in a freehold. It affirms that the prime award of labour is not economic.

THE HARVEST

At the Springhead Festival described above, the Harvest Home was timed to follow immediately on the Harvest Thanksgiving—a practice introduced in Victorian times when the farmhouse suppers had disappeared and the farmers and their men met after service to carouse in a big tent or barn. It was then many centuries since the English Church had taken an interest in the harvest. Once she had welcomed it with a peal of bells, blessed its "creatures" of wheat and bread, and permitted a corn puppet to be fixed above the chancel arch, probably because it had been fixed in the pagan temple that first occupied the site. There the straw manikin gradually straightened itself into the form of a cross. But the Reformation swept all this away. The puppets lingered in a handful of churches, but the creatures were no longer blessed. The eighteenth century Church cared little or nothing for the harvest, and we owe our Thanksgiving Service to Hawker of Morwenstow, it seems. In the Summer of 1843 he issued a notice to his flock, inviting them to receive the Sacrament on the following Sunday "in the bread of the new corn", reviving in this way the habit of ancient Lammas, though later in the season; and it is clear from his wording that the notion would be novel to his parishioners, if not to himself. Writing thirty years later, his biographer observed that "there is scarcely a church in England in which a Harvest Thanksgiving Service is not held".* This continues to be true. Thanksgiving is generally at evensong, but of course the decorations have been there throughout the day from early Eucharist, and with the co-operation of some more of our Anglo-Catholic friends the idea of a Thanksgiving Communion might become popular. Whether we owe the decorations also to Hawker of Morwenstow is not certain, but it may well be so, for he was fond of embellishing his

* S. Baring-Gould, *The Vicar of Morwenstow*, 1876, p. 226.

church on the Cornish cliffs, even on quite unecclesiastical occasions like Midsummer.

Blood-dark dahlias, bronze corn-coloured chrysanthemums, mauve Michaelmas daisies—these are the flowers that wrangle with the loud saints above them in hot-coloured jubilation. Bunches of grapes hang from the pulpit over bowing sheaves, or from the lectern, where wheat and barley are crossed under the golden bird. Around the font, and along the window ledges, and each side of the chancel steps, there are pools and tumuli of apples, melons, plums and peaches; potatoes, turnips and cucumbers; baskets of figs, currants, raspberries and nuts; great dropsical marrows; and loaves of bread confessing to sheaves. And all these have been sent by parishioners, and will afterwards be given to the hospitals or distributed in local charity. As at Christmas, it would be interesting to attempt in some part of the church a more formal treatment than is customary—say a strict pyramid or cone of fruits on the font, crisp and regular as those seen on the hands of worshippers in certain Egyptian wall-reliefs, but larger. In the corn lands the "Corn Baby" might be revived, not necessarily as a doll, but as a formal device, something ingenious and beautiful, worked from the best ears of that harvest, and hung up prominently in the church.* This festival remains one of the best attended in the English sacred year, with its air of earth-loving generosity, and with its solid and eminently singable hymns.

* Whalton in Northumberland and Little Waltham in Essex are two villages where a Corn Baby may still be found, and there are several others. The last ears are dressed like a doll in coloured paper, with head and hands formed by the ears bursting from neck and sleeves. Sometimes the frilled skirt is white and bound with a yellow sash—like that of the girl-Ceres on the leading horse, mentioned in p. 188—but the colour changes year by year. Afterwards this moppet is taken to church and fastened to the back of a pew.

Then at Overbury, on Bredon, a charmingly formal twisted cone or obelisk has been hung each year in the church porch, and smaller pyramids have been taken into the houses. Then again at Great Bardfield, near Braintree, three devices are hung in the church every year, representing 'Faith', 'Hope' and 'Charity', each woven out of wheat, oats and barley: a Cross on the pulpit, an Anchor and a Heart on the pillars of the screen. Moreover the conception seems to be modern, though the craft is traditional, and it was only in 1938 that they were introduced into the church for Harvest Thanksgiving, by the present Vicar, who reports: "I think the people now expect to see them.' Mr. Fred Mizen, of Great Bardfield, the creator of these, has also made some more formal devices, and so has Mr. Sid Boatman of Debden in the same county.

But indeed the Corn Spirit has many likenesses. His wheat-stalk image still appears on the gables of thatched farm houses as a cross, a cock, an apple, a crown, a boat, or simply as a finial of straw. It is seldom seen any longer on the ricks themselves.

The Hay Harvest, earlier in the year, was formerly another occasion for song, dance and carousal, now extinct. See *Country Life,* June 27th, 1947.

MICHAELMAS DAY

SEPTEMBER 29TH

ST. MICHAEL AND ALL ANGELS

Q. *What proof is there of the Existence of Angels?*
A. *The general Consent and Tradition of Mankind concerning it and their Ministry about us; confirmed by the clear and expressed Testimony of Scripture, which gives us an Account of their appearing to the holy Men of old.*

NELSON'S *Festivals,* 1703

AFTER the Harvest, outstanding festival of the orchards and ploughlands, Michaelmas Day appears in this century a modest occasion. It is the festival of All Angels, even as November 1st of All Saints, November 2nd of All Souls, and—if the addition is not too preposterous—even as April 1st is the festival of All Fools. But chiefly it is the feast of St. Michael, Archangel and Prince of Angels, and something must here be said of this terrific being. First, it would be well to admit that our monumental masons are too lenient with us. They offer us comfortable angels, with limp uplifted finger, submissive, mildly nightdressed. Yet when an angel was found seated by the empty sepulchre, "his countenance was like lightning and his raiment white as snow." "Every Angel is terrible," says Rilke, and indeed these citizens of a purely spiritual world have nearly always been shocking to half-animal man when they assumed a body to converse with him—shocking still, when he knew that he was destined to become their equal. Instinctively he fell flat on his face. "The countenance of an angel of God, very terrible," reported Manoah's wife, and Gideon supposed that he must die because he had seen one. To confront the Archangel Michael and survive might well be beyond human capacity. It was he who commanded in the War in Heaven, succeeding, some have supposed, to the rank and honour of the rebel Lucifer. Indeed, the lower angels are formidable enough, but at least they are "messengers" closely concerned with the doings of man. Possibly a guiding—possibly too a *mis*guiding—genius attends each soul continuously between birth and death. However that may be, the unity of men and angels, of the natural and supernatural, was celebrated on this day by those who valued it.

But in a modern book whose theme is trivial enough in comparison with these ideas, the festival can only be included on the slenderest of grounds. Michaelmas Goose still appears on the table in some houses. It was eaten this day at least as long ago as the fifteenth century, and probably much longer—ever since fat geese and the Feast of Angels have coincided—ever since a goose formed part of the Michaelmas rent. Now the meaning of the day has all but vanished; and its name is remembered chiefly on account of a flower, the Michaelmas daisy, into which is instilled the sharp and haunted, and yet affable, radiance of warm days. It was about a week beforeMichaelmas that Keats walked in the valley of the Itchen below Winchester, and returned to put on paper his ode 'To Autumn'.

ALL HALLOWS EVE

OCTOBER 31ST

And two long glasses brimmed with muscatel
Bubble upon the table. A ghost may come.
> W. B. YEATS—*All Souls' Night*

THIS was a notable occasion, the eve of the Celtic New Year, and a Festival of Fire. Pagan and Christian uses were as thickly intertwined at this season as at any in the year. Bonfires were lit to the dying sun, church bells rang throughout the night, and the future was canvassed to reveal itself in divinations, when pebbles were placed in the fire, apple peel formed initials on the floor, or when at bedtime a girl ate an apple in front of her glass, all the while combing her hair, till the ghost of her husband-to-be looked dimly in over her shoulder. The bonfires have shifted in the calendar, the bells are silenced, and superstitions are not the subject of this book; nevertheless, detached from nearly every observance, some of the ancient glamour still clings to the season of All Hallows.

Before the Reformation, two festivals composed this briefest of 'tides', the feast of All Saints on November 1st, instituted in the ninth century, and the feast of All Souls on November 2nd, introduced by the Abbot of Clugny in 998. Thus the whole company of the dead were remembered in the liturgies of the Church; and in the ignorance of the peasant home the living reached out to them, and hoped by the pressure of their willing to break down for one night the frontier fixed between two kingdoms, and enable those on the far side to return.   On All Souls Eve families sat up, and little cakes, known as Soul Cakes, were eaten by everyone. There were still a few children in 1938, going from door to door "souling" for cakes or money, by singing a song.* As the clock struck twelve there was silence, for at this hour the souls of the dead would revisit their earthly homes. There were candles burning in every room to guide them, no longer familiar with the furry darkness of 'Middle Earth', and there was a glass of wine on the table to refresh them.   But even though the room became crowded with urgent invisible faces, no one looked for the wine to diminish by even a hair's breadth during the vigil,

> "For it is a ghost's right,
> His element is so fine
> Being sharpened by his death,
> To drink from the wine breath
> While our gross palates drink from the whole
> wine."†

It need hardly be said that authority for all this was never found in the doctrines of the Church. She simply decreed that on these two days the faithful should remember the mystical union—spiritual *nearness* indeed—of the dead and the living. And yet not "simply" either, for the season was largely determined by the now familiar strategy. We remember in Homer how the dead could only squeak like bats, till Odysseus offered them blood to drink. The custom of putting out drink for the dead on this night is probably as old as that, or older. It was above all others the time of

* A. R. Wright and T. E. Lones, *British Calendar Customs: England,* 1936–8, Vol. III.
† W. B. Yeats, 'All Souls' Night,' Collected Poems.

spirit-walkings, and thus the reverse of unhaunted Christmas;
the time of the Witches' Sabbath and Black Mass, and of much
supernatural traffic, with good or evil import not clearly
determined.

The reformers of the Church of England affirmed that they
were Catholics. Their aim was to restore belief to its early
purity. Thus they retained the Feast of All Saints in the
Calendar, but removed the Feast of All Souls, because it
encouraged ideas of the dead that were entirely unchristian.
For this reason these atavistic ideas perished rather early in
England. The 'Hallow E'en' games, also of immense
antiquity, lasted a while longer, and seem to have been
played in the middle of the last century. They mostly
involved the eating of apples and nuts—nuts which the Roman
boys had played with at this season, and which gave to this
evening the name of "Nut-crack Night" in the North. There
were chestnuts roasting in the embers, an omen in every
pop and leap. There was "bobbing for apples" in a tub of
water: trying, that is, to catch them in the mouth without
help of hands. Then there was the stick revolving on a
twisted thread with an apple at one end and a lighted candle
at the other. The children stood in a circle beneath it,
hands tied behind backs, and jumped in turn to grab the
apple with their teeth. In this game bad timing was apt to
singe the hair and splash the face with candlegrease.

'Hallow E'en' dances and children's parties are still
moderately popular, and in their preparation the quality
of the night should be remembered, and something of its
import. It is Winter's Eve, for traditionally the dark
season begins on the morrow, November 1st, and as yet
there is no thought of Christmas. The room should be
candlelit, but not with the brilliance and purity of Candlemas, that earliest allusion to Spring. Here the effect is

rather of mystery, and the lighting should perhaps be a little obscure. Dark-coloured candles could be used, and others might be placed in fantastic lanterns, carved out of mangolds. Such were the lanterns quite recently made by the children of Hinton St. George, and carried about on this night with singing.

On All Souls' Day the living pray for the dead, affirming the unity of souls from one end of time to the other. Now that superstition is no longer a real danger, the Feast has been restored to the Church of England's Calendar in the Prayer Book of 1928.

GUY FAWKES DAY

"Video Rideo"

IT was in the last week of October, 1605—ten days before
the opening of Parliament—that the Roman Catholic Lord
Monteagle received an anonymous letter. Suggestively,
melodramatically indeed, it told him, "they shall receyve a
terrible blowe, this parleament, and yet they shall not seie
who hurts them." For himself, however, "the dangere is
passed as soon as yowe have burnt the letter."

The writer would seem to have misjudged his man. Lord
Monteagle did not burn the letter, he at once showed it to
Lord Salisbury. At Court, opinions are said to have been
divided. Some may have thought it the work of a madman,
but others, including the King, were suspicious; and in fact
they arrived at a fairly accurate idea of what was afoot.
However, the Council determined to make no search until
the day before the opening so that the plot—whatever it
might be—should be perfected. And thus, alarmed though
they were at the possibility of a leakage, the conspirators
met a few days later and decided to proceed. Then, on
November 4th, the Lord Chamberlain and Monteagle made
their search. Inside one cellar, rented by a Roman Catholic
called Percy, they came upon a sinister figure—afterwards
they described him as "a very bad and desperate fellow"—
who gave his name as Johnson and declared that he was
Percy's servant. They made no comment, and passed on.
The cellar seemed to be very full of wood.

Guy Fawkes was now seriously disturbed. He and his fellow-conspirators, all men of good family, Catesby, Tresham, Percy, and the rest, most of them converts and with the fervour of converts, had been working for more than a year on this, the most ambitious plot in our history, to destroy the structure of Protestant England in one instant, the King and the Royal Family, the Bishops, Judges and Nobility. A ton and a half of gunpowder had been in Percy's cellar for nearly six months; and Fawkes had been given the task of setting it off, because of his unshakable nerve and resolution. Unfortunately for them the conspirators felt that they must warn some of the Roman Catholic peers: hence their ruin. For either the letter to Monteagle was a genuine warning, or else it was inspired by a Government already informed of the design through similar warnings. Now the conspirators were all leaving London, and Fawkes was alone. He had his slow fuse: that would give him a quarter of an hour to get clear of the building and lose himself in the streets. A boat was waiting on the river. As soon as that prodigious and gratifying roar overtook him, he was to make all speed to Flanders and there spread the news of the assassination. A regiment was waiting only for that signal to embark for England. At the same time the Duke of York, afterwards Charles I, was to be captured—it was thought that he would not attend the Opening of Parliament—and the revolutionary Government would declare that England had returned to the Old Faith. The Anglicans would be helpless, the structure of their Church and State obliterated, and the *coup d'état* would have succeeded; to be followed in due course, we may be sure, by a religious war as savage as that which retarded the development of Germany for two hundred years.

About midnight, returning to the cellar, Fawkes was

suddenly confronted by a small posse of men headed by a Westminster magistrate, and he knew that he was lost. The cellar was opened; the wood tossed aside; and one after another all of his thirty-six barrels of gunpowder, so often inspected for damp, so carefully tended so long, were revealed in the light of their lanterns. Guy Fawkes remained admirably cool while they bound him, and removed his now almost pantomime properties: the dark lantern, and the three matches, or fuses. He said it was not God who had given him away, but the Devil. He said if the magistrate had caught him inside the cellar he would have "blown him up, house, himself, and all". They bound him and led him away, and at one in the morning he found himself in the King's bedchamber, facing the Government.

Calm as ever, he refused to make any statement, except that his name was Johnson, and that he wished the plot had succeeded. When the King asked him if he did not regret his attempt to murder the Royal Family, he replied that a desperate disease called for a desperate remedy—adding insolently that "one of his objects was to blow the Scots back again into Scotland". The same night he was removed to the Tower, and there for the next few days he was continually questioned by the judges Popham and Coke, some of the questions being prepared by the King himself; and still he would not talk. Then he was threatened with torture, and that, too, had no effect. Then he was tortured, his body stretched on the rack, each heightening of the tension accompanied by the promise of instant relief if he would confess, and inevitably there came the moment when he could bear no more. Lifted from the machine, he described the entire plot, though still without giving any names—or still, as they put it, "stubborn and perverse." Next day, in the face of further torture, he broke down completely and told all. With a shaking hand he signed his confession, "Guido Fawkes."

In the meantime Parliament had assembled in a mood compounded of intense relief, loyalty and indignation. They ordered that November the Fifth should be observed as a holiday for ever. They ordered a special service to be prepared, and this remained in the English Prayer Book for over two hundred years. Printing presses were put to work to make all the capital they could out of a national escape richly enhanced with the trappings of melodrama. The title page of a memorial Prayer Book depicts the Eye of God directing a timely rapier of light at the approaching vileness of a tip-toe assassin, a symbol repeated in many engravings, sometimes with the words" Video Rideo"—"I see and smile"— written along the beam. There had been no such excitement in England since all the hill-tops had caught fire for the Armada. But it was not until January 31st that five of the conspirators were brought to a scaffold opposite the building they would surely have demolished but for an error in judgement. Guy Fawkes was the last to mount.—Death by hanging, let us note: not by burning, as popular custom might lead us to suppose. He was ill, for the torture had broken him, and he had to be helped up the ladder. He spoke briefly, asking the King and the State to forgive him.

We cannot fail to respect him for his devotion to the cause, and his loyalty to his friends. For their sakes he invited torture, and withstood it for a time beyond which few would care to hold out. Honour was well satisfied there. Then perhaps we ought to respect him for his action too, remembering that he lived in an age when many Christians believed that the faith might be preserved by violent means. But no, the design was too furtive, too indiscriminately murderous: we will not condone it. Yet the conspirators attended Mass together in secret, and we may suppose that Fawkes died with what he believed to be a clear conscience. So far from rebutting the suggestion, his final words support it. He wished to die in charity with all men.

So it was that England, even in the act of discarding the festivals and gaieties of a thousand years—they fell out of English life in the seventeenth century as the hair falls out in a grave illness—acquired an unexpected and most popular holiday. A valid excuse had been found for what, after all, the young enjoy in all ages: for going in procession; for bright lights and songs; and for the rapture of destroying something. Puritans could hardly condemn a frolic so odious to the Scarlet Woman, and in fact they often approved of it. For Calvinistic eyes on any hill-top that evening, in the years that followed, there must have been a gladdening spectacle. It must have seemed as if the rising spiritual heat against Rome had broken out into points of physical fire all over the purified and now darkening landscape.

Certainly that Protestant heat was enough to make the day popular in many of our towns. So great was it in Lewes, where in Queen Mary's reign seventeen Protestants had been burnt alive, that its glow has not abated to this day. Relit in 1945, after six Novembers of compulsory darkness, the torches and bonfires once again filled the streets of Lewes with an immense number of townspeople and visitors. The four 'Bonfire Societies' carried their Guys in procession, fancy dress was worn, the ancient 'No Popery' banners were upraised, and some of the speeches delivered over the doomed conspirator were of a flavour only a degree less Protestant. Similar junketings were revived at Battle, and at Bridgwater in Somerset, where the brutal suppression of Monmouth's rebellion is not forgotten. In 1946 the celebrations at Battle were more elaborate than any within recent memory.

Indeed, in its present well-nourished form, it is comparatively modern. The 'Societies' of Lewes and the organising Committee of Bridgwater were formed in the last century to prevent disorders, and it is they who have transformed a riot into a carnival. Popular demonstrations tend, in our time, either to die out or to become 'official'—that is to say, more formal and elaborate, and of course, less dangerous. The bonfires are no longer lit in the streets, but at a safe remove, and last year young men were arrested in a large number of country towns for throwing squibs among the crowd in the ancient manner. For of course Lewes and Bridgwater are not unique; but elsewhere the impetus derived from religious zeal has long since decayed. Sometimes Fawkes himself has been forgotten, in spite of the rhyme, and a more contemporary villain has found his way to the flames. Thus, through a century and a half, November the Fifth has provided an amusing commentary on the changing hatreds of the English people. 'Boney' was burnt, time and again; so, too, was Cardinal Wiseman, first Archbishop of Westminster; and Nana Sahib of the Cawnpore atrocities; and the Turkish Sultan of the Armenian atrocities; and Kruger; and the Kaiser; and Hitler. And it is interesting to remember that during the Pacifist 1920's a band of ex-Servicemen more than once hoisted on to the faggots the effigy of 'War'.

And yet the bonfires of November the Fifth may be older even than Guido himself, and measurelessly older. The writer believes that when the people of England lit their fires and danced about them, it was no new thing: some of them had done this all their lives, only they had done it five nights earlier, on October 31st. For others, the *memory* of a ritual fire at All Hallows might be fresh enough to revive the practice. Certain features of local observance lend weight to the theory of a ritual origin and remind us of Midsummer Eve. In a number of places no Guy was burnt: only a great fire was lit. In some, when the fires died down, the young couples would begin leaping through them. In some, flaming barrels of tar were rolled from the top of a hill. Centuries before, the Christian Easter had attracted and absorbed into its major brilliance some local Spring God, slain and resurrected. So now, it would seem, did Guy Fawkes attract and give new meaning to the Hallow E'en fires. Thus it may have come to pass that though in the flesh he was hanged, in effigy he has always been *burnt*. Without the fires, Fawkes would hardly have remained so famous a national villain. Without Fawkes the fires would have vanished. As it is, we appear to keep on November the Fifth the one surviving Festival of Fire in our country.*

Ceremonies of the people die first in the minds of grown men and women. Children cherish them for a while but lack the mental stamina to keep up observances which are delightful only in the degree that they are exacting, and gradually the custom corrupts. So it is with Guy Fawkes Night. Except in a few towns and villages it is now honoured in a very half-hearted way by small children who are merely bent on collecting pennies. Often they have the impertinence to beg "A penny for the old Guy" when no guy exists, and all they can produce, on demand, is a member of their party with his face blacked! Sussex and Somerset apart, Guy Fawkes is in a decline.

* In support of this theory we may note that it is extremely difficult to introduce an invented custom at any time. On the other hand, it is not certain that the Hallows Eve bonfires were widely remembered in the seventeenth century.

Yet the custom has much to recommend it. It gives pleasure to children, and it encourages them once again in the dying year of the spirit to create their own enjoyment, even as they should have created it out of the paper-chains of Christmas, when the festive year was young. Most of us remember from childhood the Autumn fires which seemed, with the robin's song in ruined gardens, to mark the death of Summer. A bonfire has thus a symbolic value: it points a finger to a new place in the text of living from which our attention can so easily wander. All children are attracted to a fire out of doors, and will stand for a long while fascinated by its behaviour in the wind, which gives the flames a variety of brief forms, like flowing water, or combed-out hair, or wild, transparent grass. And this, the best of all bonfires, belongs aptly enough to the weakest point in our rather impoverished cycle of festivities—in the middle of the monotonous stretch between Harvest and Christmas, a stretch once interrupted by the magic uses of All Hallows Eve. May it therefore come to pass that when Hitler is as dusty a hobgoblin as Bonaparte, the ritual flames will still be snapping at the heels of a Guy; and a Guy, let us add, decently dressed for the occasion.

To be really effective he must be nearly life-size. His body should be made of old clothes stuffed with straw into the shape of limbs, and he should have a pole for a spine. On top of the pole his head will be placed. This should be a mangel-wurzel, hollowed out and also filled, but not too tightly, with straw soaked in paraffin. Holes should be cut for eyes so that when the straw in the skull catches fire they may appear to smoke and glow with diabolical rage. A face should be painted, or better still, a terrible mask made out of *papier-mâché* and wired to the head so that it cannot fall away in burning. Alternatively, a

THE GUY.

Equipped with his traditional 'properties'.

Drawing by Robin Jaques.

Catherine-wheel can be fixed to each eye, and in the mouth a Golden Fountain or some other firework which gushes out in a sheaf of sparks and flame; and if the flames fail to light them, these can be lit with a torch. On his head there should be a tall pointed hat, of paper if necessary, and if possible a wig. His hands will be merely stuffed-out gloves, but one hand will grasp—or this Guy is degenerate—the "dark lantern", and the other the "three matches". These, of course, will be fireworks of the indoor kind, which go off in the midst of tingling sparks.

There are two ways of burning the Guy. One is to strap him high up on a stick which has already been driven into the ground, and then to pile the faggots up to his feet. Both grander and simpler is the other and more ancient way: to tie him in an old chair, slide two poles under the seat, and carry him in procession, accompanied by flaming torches and scattered squibs (Bridgwater squibs are formidable; so are "Lewes Rousers" and "Battle Rousers"), to the place of execution, where a great mound of faggots is already prepared, and he is merely hoisted on top and the legs of the chair driven firmly in. Whichever method is chosen he should be tied with string and not with wire, so that in the end end he may break loose and topple dreadfully into the flames.

Still, there remains a possible objection to be considered. It might be that a yearly reminder of Protestant rage against Roman Catholic misdoing would inflame the hatred of both parties. If it were true that Englishmen are more divided because of a bonfire and a figure of straw and rags, there would now be a reason why gunpowder treason should be forgot. But who seriously believes that they are, even in Lewes? We know that the body of a custom may live when the informing spirit has expired. We may deplore this at Christmas, but we find it quite satisfactory on May Day.

So it may be on November the Fifth. And if we must remember the iniquity of one Roman Catholic, let us not forget that, but for the wisdom and loyalty of another, the thirty-six barrels would have done their monstrous work.

ST. CECILIA'S DAY

NOVEMBER 22ND

When music sounds, gone is the earth I know,
And all her lovely things even lovelier grow;
Her flowers in vision flame, her forest trees
Lift burdened branches, stilled with ecstasies.

WALTER DE LA MARE—'*Music*'

In 1945 it would have been fanciful to include St. Cecilia's Day among the English Festivals. In 1947 it would be unimaginative to leave it out. If this charming day, twice cared for in England and twice almost forgotten, should come into public remembrance for a third time, the year recorded in musical history will be 1946.

Cecilia is the patron saint of music. Saints, it is true, have sometimes only a slender connection with the arts and festivals they patronise:—St. Valentine now blesses a telegraph form. Music may have meant very little to the girl who died for her faith in the second century; or again she may well have been noted for her singing. Legends are not invariably false. At least it is certain that in giving a *name* to a festival a saint has given something of value: an excuse, an inspiration, and a human interest. The festive kite sails farther and farther from the hand that holds it, but the hand remains, none the less.

The researches of de Rossi* have confirmed what Fortunatus, Bishop of Poitiers, declared to be true in the sixth century: that Cecilia suffered martyrdom in Sicily, about the year 176, during the second terror imposed by

* *Roma Sotteranea*, II, 147.

H

the high-minded Marcus Aurelius. But it is the saint of the legend who has conferred a blessing on music. She was Roman, we read, born nobly, and born a Christian. She was given in marriage to a young pagan whose name was Valerian, but she had privately taken a vow of virginity. On her wedding night she revealed this to him as tenderly as she could, not forgetting to add that she was often visited by an angel, who would certainly strike him dead if he molested her. Valerian received this news unfavourably, yet loved her enough to seek baptism. Returning, he found his wife in conversation with the angel, who thereupon crowned them with flowers—with lilies and roses, picked in no earthly garden. It must have been Winter; for when Valerian's brother entered the room he remarked on the overwhelming fragrance that filled it; but to him the floral crowns were invisible. He too was baptised; and in course of time the brothers were martyred. Then Cecilia was put to the question, and condemned to be roasted to death in a dry bath. All night and all the following day she reclined there, miraculously cool, and at last an executioner was sent to cut off her head. The operation horribly miscarried, and it was three days before the girl bled to death, still gay at heart, and encouraging her companions.

That is the story that Chaucer tells, with customary grace, in the Second Nun's Tale. It may be asked in what manner the saint was connected with music, and the answer, such as it is, will only be found in one couplet:

> And whil the organs maden melodie
> To God allone in hertè thus sang she.

On that couplet, or rather on the equivalent words in the Golden Legend, Cecilia's musical reputation must stand.

At any rate it was thought to be well established in the
Middle Ages, when the guilds of musicians adopted her as
their patron saint. She was even supposed to have invented
the instrument named in her legend, and thereby to have
"added length to solemn sounds", as Dryden puts it. Thus,
though Domenichino portrays her fingering a lute before an
enraptured cherub, in Raphael's masterpiece she is seen
accompanying herself at a small portable organ. She has
been much painted and praised.

But in England she was forced to withdraw her patronage
at the Reformation. It was enlisted again, to protect the
art against an absurd opinion to which the Reformation had
ultimately led. The Puritans had declared all music, whether
sacred or secular, to be dangerous fare, if not indeed "a cup
of poyson to all the world"; and that opinion had survived
the Commonwealth. 'The Musical Society' was formed in
1683, partly to keep St. Cecilia's Day in a worthy manner.
Each year, on November 22nd, the Society attended a
service in London, generally at St. Bride's, to enjoy, by way
of text and illustration, a sermon preached in defence of
cathedral music, and an Anthem newly written for the
Festival. Sacred harmonies being vindicated, the congregation moved to a City company's hall, where, before
banqueting well, they were entertained by the performance
of an Ode.

The composer at the first Festival was Henry Purcell;
and it was he who in 1692 presented a magnificent Ode with
workmanlike but wingless words by Nicolas Brady. Yet on
occasion the words might be more buoyant than the music.
Dryden's 'Song for St. Cecilia's Day', set by Draghi, was
performed in 1686, and then, for 1697, reconstructed in
the form of 'Alexander's Feast' with music by Jeremiah
Clarke—a great poem, long afterwards given a worthy

setting by Handel. Indeed both poems are admirable, not only for their purpose, but in themselves.

> From harmony, from heavenly harmony
> This universal frame began.

> From harmony to harmony
> Through all the compass of the notes it ran,
> The diapason closing full in man.

Organ music is heard: cherubs by Grinling Gibbons are discovered riding out the gales of it, borne up on cushions of sound.—Yet Dryden's 'architecture', his weight and breadth, suggest Bach rather than Purcell, and Kent rather than Wren.

> So when the last and dreadful hour
> This crumbling pageant shall devour,
> The trumpet shall be reared on high
> And Music shall untune the sky.

Thus ends the 'Song'; and when Dryden rewrote it as 'Alexander's Feast' he exploited to the full, like no English poet before him, the almost hypnotic effect of verbal repetition; a technique afterwards employed by Poe in 'The Bells', but with less judgement.

Whenever the saint of harmony has been honoured in England, the English poets have been there to pay their tribute and record the fact: first Chaucer; then Dryden, followed by Pope in 1708, with his 'Ode for Music on St. Cecilia's Day'.

> By the heroes' armed shades
> Glittering through the gloomy glades,
> By the youths that died for love
> Wandering in the myrtle grove.

It may be that a third Cecilian age will inspire poetry no less distinguished. The second came to an end about the middle of the eighteenth century.* Although, since then, there have been occasional Odes by Parry, Samuel Wesley and others; although the Worshipful Company of Musicians have now for some time attended Evensong at St. Paul's on November 22nd, and although an attempt was made to revive the Festival about half a century ago; yet there has been no Festival worthy of note, for the simple reason that we have lacked, until the present period, enough composers of outstanding merit to make one. Nor was there any outward sign of this new and likelier revival before 1942.

Whether by divine dispensation or by happy coincidence, St. Cecilia's Day is Mr. Benjamin Britten's birthday, and in 1942 he revived the practice of composing an Ode in her honour. But Sir Henry Wood had already wished to recreate the Festival, and had he lived he would have been pleased by the events that took place on her day in 1946, thanks to the initiative of the *Daily Herald*. There was first a public luncheon at which the Prime Minister spoke and the Poet Laureate recited a poem. Then the Lord Mayor attended a service in St. Sepulchre's; and finally in the evening—main event of the day—there was a concert of English music at the Albert Hall, at which the Queen and Princess Elizabeth were present. Two orchestras took part, the London Philharmonic and the London Symphony, together with the Alexandra Choir. After an initial fanfare of trumpets in honour of the Fallen, works by Purcell, Elgar, Vaughan

* The Festival was kept for twenty years, with only three lapses, but after 1703 the celebrations were very infrequent. Among the poets who contributed Odes were Dryden, Congreve, Shadwell, D'Urfey, Hughes, and afterwards Pope. Among the composers who put them to music were Purcell, Blow, Draghi, Eccles, Jeremiah Clarke, and afterwards Handel. Pope's fine though imitative Ode was not given a setting until 1730. (See Grove's *Dictionary of Music*, article on St. Cecilia.)

[217]

Williams, Walton, and other Englishmen were heard—including the Overture to Purcell's Ode of 1692, and including, in the best traditional manner, certain music composed for the occasion.*

As private patronage dwindles the arts become increasingly sensitive to the moods of authority. It is not without value when a Prime Minister and a Lord Mayor consent to give some of their many official minutes to the recognition of music. The revival of St. Cecilia's Day is appropriate, for English music is in better health than at any time since the Commonwealth, and music is the most social of the arts, and indeed the one art that has anything to gain from an annual celebration. But whether the events of last November will be often repeated, whether the custom will extend to other towns, and to private rooms where musicians gather to make music, as the seventeenth-century custom extended to Oxford, Salisbury, Winchester and Gloucester—whether St. Cecilia's Day is really to be included among the Festivals —are questions that cannot be answered at the present time.

* Programme by Odham's Press. Notices in *The Times*, November 22nd and 23rd, 1946.

THE WHEEL OF LIFE

But man is a Noble Animal, splendid in ashes, and pompous in the grave, solemnising Nativities and Deaths with equal lustre, nor omitting Ceremonies of bravery, in the infamy of his nature.
SIR THOMAS BROWNE—*Urne-Burial*

A HUNDRED years ago it would still have been appropriate to write at some length of those ceremonies which mark, not an event in the year of the Church, nor a season in the natural year, nor a day of popular amusement, but a stage in the unfolding of a single life. To-day there is less that need be said of these events in a book of this kind, either because no customs remain to be described—and that is true of pregnancy, and the day of birth, and the 'churching' of women—or because the customs are too stereotyped to be altered at will, and perhaps too familiar to be worth describing in detail. This appears to be the case where a betrothal, a wedding, a christening and a death are concerned. When we have mentioned the engagement ring, what else remains to be said of a modern betrothal? Yet birth, love and death have not been deprived of their customs because we no longer consider them important, but for an opposite reason. They are so near to us that we can only allow them a *social* celebration of a very attenuated and conventional sort. To our ancestors we should seem, no doubt, excessively private and self-conscious; but civilisation has made us nice. We could not tolerate the frank amusements of a Tudor wedding night, or the feasting after an ancient funeral. The last to surrender these joys have been the poorest, but surrendered they are or shortly will be. Few Cockneys are as pompous in the grave as their great-grandfathers, accompanied there by a train of spanking carriages, or, being left in the cemetry, as splendidly productive of good cheer in others. In a world of sophistication, Hymen is modest and Mors stark, and both are inviolable in privacy. We must confine our attention to the three occasions which are still enjoyable, and still, in greater or less degree, kept up with ceremony.

CHRISTENINGS

How but in custom and in ceremony
Are innocence and beauty born?
Ceremony's a name for the rich horn
And custom for the spreading laurel tree.

W. B. YEATS—*A Prayer for my Daughter*

MANY parents who bring their children to be baptised
to-day could be accused of frivolity. For either they inwardly
endorse the statement "All this I steadfastly believe", when
they do not, or they refuse to endorse it, and render their
presence in the church ridiculous—though not, of course,
the presence of the child! No social benefit accrues from
baptism. Why then do they come? Perhaps ordinary
degrees of scepticism never *quite* allay the suspicion that
there may, after all, be some mysterious virtue in it.
Baptism—the giving of a name—has been for so long an
event of supreme importance that a sense of this may well
have become instinctive, quite apart from belief. Thus the
event bristled with omens. It could not be otherwise, for
in receiving a name the infant was understood to receive a
self, to become, finally, unique and distinct. To some, the
statements of Dr. Jung are more palatable than those of the
Common Prayer Book. "Let us not forget", he says,* "that
what the Christian Sacrament of baptism purports to do is of
the greatest importance for the psychic development of
mankind. Baptism endows the human being with a unique
soul. I do not mean, of course, the baptismal rite in itself as
a magical act that is effective at one performance. I mean

* *Modern Man in Search of a Soul*, 1941, Ch. VII, p. 167.

[221]   H*

that the idea of baptism lifts a man out of his archaic identification with the world and changes him into a being who stands above it."

The event is still celebrated at home, however informally, and in many families a Christening Cake is not forgotten. It was once the rule on this occasion for Godparents to present the child with a set of twelve silver Apostle Spoons, or if they were poor, with one—bearing, of course, the image of the apostle after whom the child was named, worked at the top of the handle. Silver spoons were still given in the nineteenth century, though no longer with imagery. To-day, too, a christening present is commonly of silver, knife and spoon and fork, mug, or napkin ring, engraved with the name and a date, but perhaps equally often a gift of some other kind, of which, after all, nothing can be firmly stated except that it is supposed to be one of a lasting sort.

WEDDINGS

Things, composed of such flimsy Materials as the Fancies of a Multitude, do not seem calculated for a long Duration; yet have these survived shocks, by which even Empires have been overthrown.

JOHN BRAND—*Observations on Popular Antiquities*

THERE was once a Christian country that abolished the sacrament of marriage. Henceforth, the government decreed, no priest shall be required to officiate. It was the government of England in 1653, and not long afterwards a union in the new mode was recorded at Chalgrave in Bedfordshire: the intention of the couple being three times published "in one parish meeting house called the church and no exception made against it, the said Henry Fisher and Sarah Newson were married XXIX Sept by Francis Anteres Esq and in the presence of Will. Martin and Abraham Newson." The prosaic pages of a Parish Register will sometimes reflect the mood of a nation. All the revulsion from those negative years can be sensed in another entry. It is the comment of the priest or clerk at Launceston in Cornwall, inserted after the Restoration on an earlier page: "Hereafter follow marriages by laymen, according to the prophanes, and giddyness of the times, without precedent or example in any Christian kingdom or Commonwealth, from the birth of Christ unto this very year 1655."

Only a part of our marriage customs can have been withheld in this interlude, too brief and too unpopular to eradicate any. Most that we now keep up were already antique at the time of the Commonwealth; though one at least is more recent—the honeymoon. It may be of interest to examine the antiquity of each, and to record a few of those that have fallen by the way, for to record them all would demand a complete chapter of folklore.

In church, the words spoken by bride and bridegroom have hardly been altered in five centuries, except that at the time of Chaucer we should have heard the bride promising to be "buxom in bed and at board".* Bridesmaids were 'bridemaids', but their function was to attend the *bridegroom* to church, while the 'bridegroom men'—antecedent to the 'best man'—escorted the bride. She was garlanded in any century of which we have record, though her wreath of mock orange must be comparatively recent, an emblem of fertility out of Moorish Spain or the Holy Land. Her gold ring is equally immemorial, a token of the eternal and the incorruptible. Round the inside a 'posy' was often engraved: "pure and endless," for example—Bewick would engrave not a few in his 'prentice days—and according to general belief a little artery ran from the fourth finger of the left hand directly to the heart. It is curious to reflect that the Puritans strove to abolish a device that is to-day so much the symbol of a vow, and not, at times, without a certain restraining influence.

That there was music need hardly be said; wedding music long before Wagner and Mendelssohn provided their hackneyed alternatives, from which—may we hope?—we are beginning to escape. In the country the young men took part in a race, and the winner was entitled to untie the bride's garters, or else there was a general scramble to remove them in the church itself. Then was there indeed

* She would have said that in the *porch* however, where ordinary people had been married from the earliest times. Witness the Wife of Bath: "Housbondes at churché dore she haddé fyve."

"such a lyftinge up and discouering of the damsels clothes" as scandalised Miles Coverdale. When, in a more genteel society, the country brides began blushingly to offer ribbons to be run for, it was the turn of the young men to be scandalised. In the afterglow, we still kiss the bride in the vestry.

At the church door she was showered with rose petals, and with wheat that she might be fruitful, later with rice, later still with paper confetti, introduced within living memory; and flowers or rushes were strewn in her path. At her own door the bridegroom lifted her across the threshold, not at all to master a feigned reluctance, but to protect her against magic, always thick in doorways. Then followed the Bride Ale, longer and more convivial than the modern reception. Presents were given, but only, until the nineteenth century, by the nearest relatives, and by husband and wife to one another. 'Wedding cake' was 'bride cake', originally made of symbolic wheat or barley. Bride and bridegroom kissed above it, and she must cut it herself, or be childless. And even as now, all who wished them luck must eat.

So the hour arrived when the couple must be brought to their room, with lights and laughter. The bride was undressed by her maids and put to bed while the men were undressing her husband, whom they presently led in. Even then they were not released, for late into the night a ballad might be struck up at the door, or 'rough music' break out below the window. And next morning there was music again when the company broke in to greet them, and learned how handsome a present the bridegroom had determined in the interval to bestow on his bride.

After this manner might be performed the nuptials of a Tudor yeoman. Higher and lower in the social scale we should have encountered other degrees of candour and ceremonial, and of course no allowance has been made, in so brief an account, for local variations in custom. The yeoman was at the centre of English society, almost the representative Englishman, constantly praised for his solid worth, independent spirit and good nature, in centuries when praise of the countryman was quite untinged with sentimentality. And if the wedding customs of his betters were less bucolically crude, they were hardly less arduous. Delicacy apart, few couples to-day could support the strain of such an ordeal. As the refinement of manners proceeded it became increasingly distasteful, and according to Fielding it was "to spare the ladies' blushes" that the modern honeymoon was introduced: an escape into privacy—or partial privacy at least, for, to begin with, the bride was accompanied and supported by one of her friends.

BIRTHDAYS

*To have been made in human form is ever a cause for rejoicing;
and beyond this are the numberless transitions leading to perfec-
tion. Is not this unspeakable bliss?*

CHWANG TSZE—*The Nan Hwa Classic*

IN the course of three dilapidating centuries the charms
of a birthday have faded remarkably little, if indeed they have
faded at all, and not, on the contrary, rather enhanced
themselves where the young are concerned. For them,
Christmas alone among festivals can be said to surpass it in
potency. The old uses are well kept up. Lamb, it is true,
speaks of "the cake and orange" as if they were the special
properties of a childish birthday, and we seem to have
forgotten the orange. But that is a trifle, for the cake
survives. And yet, to say that it merely "survives" is to
imply a tentative and pleading sort of diuturnity, poorly
suggestive of the pink and glimmering, robustly contemporary object that is so much the focus of attention that it
virtually becomes the thing which it boldly, in scrawled
icing sugar, professes to be—"A Happy Birthday". And name
or initial leave us no room to question whose. When the
children enter the room the candles are already alight,
floating above the table cloth in a ring of moderate brilliance,
revealing the pyramid of presents beside one plate, done up
in coloured or tissue paper and tied with tinsel string. The
flames are white, but not piercingly so. They seem to give
out more radiance than they contain in themselves, and
have the quality of buds or petals rather than fire: incan-
descent anemones. Even a December teatime requires no

other light; and if there are so many candles that one circle within another has been formed on the cake, the flames lean in toward the centre, steadied and drawn upward in a cone of palpable heat. These 'Birthday Rings' are immemorial; and perhaps around the cake—such is the charming custom in certain families—a wreath of flowers or evergreens has been placed. They are the flowers of the season, and for a midwinter birthday there are the small, dark pointed leaves of the Roman Laurel to compose a classical garland. When all are seated, he or she whose birthday it is will be crowned with this garland and wear it throughout the meal, till the candles are blown out—at a single puff for good fortune—and the cake is cut.

But the birthday tea has been familiar to generations of children with little or no mutation; and even in the narrow years of war enough icing sugar may have been found in a jar to continue the legend, and enough candles preserved from an old Christmas tree to illustrate it. How long can a custom starve and live? Ten years perhaps; hardly more. If in their *total* austerity modern wars were to last as long as ancient ones, memory would cease to inspire action; there would emerge a way of life stripped clean of gestures and unfurnished; hollow as an empty room.

THE END

A TABLE TO FIND EASTER

and the other Movable Festivals described in this book, as far as the year 1975

LY=Leap Year	SHROVE TUESDAY	MOTHERING SUNDAY	PALM SUNDAY	EASTER	ROGATION SUNDAY*	WHITSUN
LY 1948	10 Feb.	7 Mar.	21 Mar.	28 Mar.	2 May	16 May
1949	1 Mar.	27 Mar.	10 Apr.	17 Apr.	22 May	5 June
1950	21 Feb.	19 Mar.	2 Apr.	9 Apr.	14 May	28 May
1951	6 Feb.	4 Mar.	18 Mar.	25 Mar.	29 Apr.	13 May
LY 1952	26 Feb	23 Mar.	6 Apr.	13 Apr.	18 May	1 June
1953	17 Feb.	15 Mar.	29 Mar.	5 Apr.	10 May	24 May
1954	2 Mar.	28 Mar.	11 Apr.	18 Apr.	23 May	6 June
1955	22 Feb.	20 Mar.	3 Apr.	10 Apr.	15 May	29 May
LY 1956	14 Feb.	11 Mar.	25 Mar.	1 Apr.	6 May	20 May
1957	5 Mar.	31 Mar.	14 Apr.	21 Apr.	26 May	9 June
1958	18 Feb.	16 Mar.	30 Mar.	6 Apr.	11 May	25 May
1959	10 Feb.	8 Mar.	22 Mar.	29 Mar.	3 May	17 May
LY 1960	1 Mar.	27 Mar.	10 Apr.	17 Apr.	22 May	5 June
1961	14 Feb.	12 Mar.	26 Mar.	2 Apr.	7 May	21 May
1962	6 Mar.	1 Apr.	15 Apr.	22 Apr.	27 May	10 June
1963	26 Feb.	24 Mar.	7 Apr.	14 Apr.	19 May	2 June
LY 1964	11 Feb.	8 Mar.	22 Mar.	29 Mar.	3 May	17 May
1965	2 Mar.	28 Mar.	11 Apr.	18 Apr.	23 May	6 June
1966	22 Feb.	20 Mar.	3 Apr.	10 Apr.	15 May	29 May
1967	7 Feb.	5 Mar.	19 Mar.	26 Mar.	30 Apr.	14 May
LY 1968	27 Feb.	24 Mar.	7 Apr.	14 Apr.	19 May	2 June
1969	18 Feb.	16 Mar.	30 Mar.	6 Apr.	11 May	25 May
1970	10 Feb.	8 Mar.	22 Mar.	29 Mar.	3 May	17 May
1971	23 Feb.	21 Mar.	4 Apr.	11 Apr.	16 May	30 May
LY 1972	15 Feb.	12 Mar.	26 Mar.	2 Apr.	7 May	21 May
1973	6 Mar.	1 Apr.	15 Apr.	22 Apr.	27 May	10 June
1974	26 Feb.	24 Mar.	7 Apr.	14 Apr.	19 May	2 June
1975	11 Feb.	9 Mar.	23 Mar.	30 Mar.	4 May	18 May

* For Ascension Day (Holy Thursday) add four days to Rogation Sunday.

CAROLS

Modern Collections with Words and Music

	Abbreviation
Carols New and Old, ed. Bramley and Stainer	CNO
The Oxford Book of Carols	OBC
The Cambridge Book of Carols	Camb.
The Cowley Carol Book (2 vols., Mowbray)	CCB
Carols of *The Year Book Press*	YBP
Twice 33 Carols, ed. Geoffrey Shaw (Hawker)	
A Collection of French Tunes, ed. Stainer	
Carols, ed. Cecil Sharp	

Nearly all the carols in the first three books are issued separately in leaflets. The CNO versions are probably the best known, yet CNO is now rather old-fashioned, and contains some very insipid specimens. OBC is good in tunes, sometimes poor in words. Camb. is a valuable small collection of the less familiar carols. On the whole, the best are the two excellent volumes of CCB. From the literary point of view see also R. L. Greene, *The Early English Carols*, 1935.

In drawing up the list below, no attempt has been made to distinguish between old and new. Pedantry apart, there are only two tests worth applying to a carol. Is it good to sing? Does it add to the festival? If it does neither, it is fit for rejection. The old are best, certainly; yet the last century and the present one have provided songs worth singing, even when not of the purest quality. The case of 'Good

CAROLS

King Wenceslas' is relevant. The writer does not share the purist's view of this carol, that the Victorian words are deplorable, and that the tune should be restored to the Spring, for which it was written. To him, the airy April words suggested in OBC are merely vapid, while the cosy Christmas story, familiar to everyone, grips the imagination and is true poetry of a humble sort. Humble it is, in this dazzling company; yet the good King passes the test. He is pleasant to sing about, and he certainly has added to Christmas.

CHRISTMAS CAROLS

VERY WELL KNOWN

God rest you, merry gentlemen	CNO	1	OBE	12
A Virgin unspotted	CNO	3		
The first Nowell	CNO	6	OBC	27
Good King Wenceslas	CNO	10		
See amid the Winter's snow	CNO	30		
We three Kings of Orient are	CNO	45	OBC	195
I saw three ships	CNO	64	OBC	18
As I sat on a sunny bank	OBC	3		
The holly and the ivy	OBC	38		
In dulci jubilo	OBC	86	CCB	12
O little town of Bethlehem	OBC	138	Eng. Hymnal. Songs of Praise.	

CHRISTMAS HYMNS

While shepherds watch
Hark the herald angels sing
O come, all ye faithful
Christians, awake
In the bleak mid-winter

LESS WELL KNOWN, AND SPECIALLY RECOMMENDED

Simpler Carols

What child is this	CNO	14		
The Coventry carol	CNO	61	OBC	22
Christmas Day is come (Irish)	OBC	6		
Come, all you worthy gentlemen	OBC	8		
On Christmas night	OBC	24		
This endris night	OBC	39		
The cherry tree carol	OBC	66		
The seven joys of Mary	OBC	70		
To-morrow shall be my dancing day	OBC	71		
Joseph dearest	OBC	77		
The Birds	OBC	105		
Angels from the realms	OBC	119		
Masters in this hall	OBC	137		
How far is it to Bethlehem?	OBC	142		
Adam lay ybounden	OBE	180 (Warlock)		
Lullay my liking	OBC	182		
I sing of a maiden	OBC	183		
All the bells of paradise	OBC	184		
Snow in the street	OBC	186		
Ding-dong merrily on high	Camb.	viii		
Past three o'clock	Camb.	xxv		
Blessed be that Maid Marie	CCB	2		
King Jesus hath a garden	CCB	Vol. 2 (better than OBC)		
Unto us is born a son	CCB	25 (OBC 92, inferior words)		
Up, good Christian folk	CCB	29		
Shepherds in the field	CCB	68		

CAROLS

Whence is that goodly fragrance	YBC (French tune)
For us a child (A round)	*Songs for all Seasons.* O.U.P.

Carols for Trained Choirs

The noble stem of Jesse	OBC 19 (Not difficult)
Sweet was the song	CBC 30 CCB 32
O little one	OBC 109
Bulalow	OBC 181 (Warlock)
Sweet baby, sleep	OBC 185
The flowering manger	YBP (3 part, Women's voices)

The holly and the ivy

        Arr. Walford Davies, 4 part (Novello)

        Arr. Rutland Boughton, 4 part (Curwen)

O little town of Bethlehem   Walford Davies (Novello)

Fantasia on Christmas Carols

        Vaughan Williams (Stainer and Bell). About 15 mins.

Ceremony of carols

        Benjamin Britten, 3 part, boy's or women's voices. (Boosey and Hawkes). 25 mins.

Secular Carols

Wassail	OBC 31
Wassail	

        Arr. Vaughan Williams, 4 part. (Stainer and Bell)

Blow, blow, thou winter wind	OBC 171 (Arne) first tune
Deck the hall	YBP (arr. C. Wood)
The twelve days of Christmas	(Various collections)
A merry Christmas (trad.)	O.U.P., 2 and 4 part

THE ENGLISH FESTIVALS

EASTER, MAY AND WHITSUN CAROLS

Now that Christmas carols are firmly re-established, it would be good if some of the others were revived, especially those that belong to Easter. They may be found in most of the collections listed above, and in a very useful ninepenny pamphlet by Percy Dearmer, part-editor of the Oxford Book, entitled *An Easter Carol Service*. (O.U.P., 1935.) "It is hoped," says the editor, "that this selection of Easter carols, with an order of service, may prove widely useful to those who wish to introduce carols at Eastertide." He suggests a dramatic use of lights—not over-dramatic, however, but to the Englishman's taste—very appropriate to Easter Eve: a dark church; the choir entering with candles, singing, but unaccompanied; the organ introduced; the altar candles lit up; then row upon row of little candles along the choir stalls. One can imagine a Midnight Mass conducted after this manner. These are the carols included in the pamphlet service:

Sans day carol	OBC	35
Gabriel's message	OBC	102
Hilariter!	OBC	96
The world itself	OBC	150
Christ the Lord is risen!	OBC	148
Athens	OBC	151

To these might be added—

This joyful Eastertide	CCB 51	OBC 152
	Also in a good 2-part version by A. E. Baker, YBP	

SELECT BIBLIOGRAPHY

ADDY, S. O.: *Household Tales and Traditional Remains*, 1895.
ANDREWS, WILLIAM: *Curious Church Customs*, 1895.
    Bygone Derbyshire, etc., 1892.
AUBREY, JOHN: *Remaines of Gentilisme and Judaisme* (published 1880).
    Miscellanies.
BARING-GOULD, SABINE: *Old Country Life*, 1890.
BAYNE-POWELL, ROSAMUND: *English Country Life in the Eighteenth Century*,
    1935.
BEDE, THE VENERABLE: *History of the Churche of Englande*. Translated:
    Thos. Stapleton, 1565.
BOUQUET, JOHN A.: *Christmas to Candlemas*, 1931.
BRAND, JOHN: *Observations on Popular Antiquities*, 1888 (incorporating Henry
    Bourne's *Antiquitates Vulgares*, 1725).
BROCK, ALAN ST. H.: *Pyrotechnics*, 1922.
CAMPBELL, MILDRED: *The English Yeoman under Elizabeth and the Early
    Stuarts*, 1942.
CAMPBELL, R. J.: *The Story of Christmas*, 1935.
CHADWICK, H. M.: *The Origin of the English Nation*, 1907.
CHAMBERS, E. K.: *English Literature at the Close of the Middle Ages*, 1945.
CHAMBERS, ROBERT: *The Book of Days*, 1862–4.
COURTNAY, MARGARET A.: *Cornish Feasts and Folk-lore*, 1890.
CRAWFORD, P.: *In England Still*, 1938.
CRIPPEN, T. G.: *Christmas and Christmas Lore*, 1923.
DACOMBE, MARIANNE R.: *Dorset Up Along and Down Along*, 1936.
DITCHFIELD, PETER H.: *Old English Customs*, 1896.
    Our English Villages, 1889.
DRAKE-CARNELL, F. J.: *Old English Customs and Ceremonies*, 1938.
FAIRFAX-BLAKEBOROUGH, J.: *Yorkshire Days and Yorkshire Ways*, 1935.
FRAZER, SIR JAMES G.: *The Golden Bough*, Third Edition, 1936.
GALES, R. L.: *Dwellers in Arcady*, 1931.
GARDINER, ROLF.: *England Herself*, 1943.
GLEESON WHITE: Article on Christmas Cards, *The Studio*. Extra number,
    1894.
GODFREY, ELIZABETH: *English Children in the Olden Time*, 1907.
GOMME, SIR GEORGE L.: *Ethnology in Folk-lore*, 1891.
HARDWICK, CHARLES: *Traditions, Superstitions and Folk-lore*, 1872.
HARTLEY, DOROTHY: *Made in England*, 1939.
HARTLEY, D. AND ELLIOTT, M.: *Life and Work of the People of England*,
    1925–31.
HENDERSON, WILLIAM: *Folk-lore in the Northern Counties*, edited 1879.
HERBERT, GEORGE: *The Country Parson*, 1652.
HERRICK, ROBERT: *Poetical Works*.
HOLE, CHRISTINA: *Traditions and Customs of Cheshire*, 1937.
    English Folklore, 1940.
    English Custom and Usage, 1941.
HONE, WILLIAM: *The Every-Day Book*, Vol. 1 and 2, 1826.
    The Table Book, 1827.
    The Year Book, 1829.
HOWITT, WILLIAM: *The Rural Life of England*, 1838. Also 2nd ed. 1840.
HULL, ELEANOR: *Folklore in the British Isles*, 1928.

JAMESON, STORM: *The Decline of Merry England*, 1930.
LEATHER, ELLA M.: *The Folklore of Herefordshire*, 1912.
LONG, GEORGE: *The Folklore Calendar*, 1930.
MARTIN, SIR THEODORE: *Life of the Prince Consort*, 1875.
MASSINGHAM, H. J.: *A Countryman's Journal*, 1939.
            Country Relics, 1939.
            Men of Earth, 1943; and other works.
OLIVIER, EDITH: *Country Moods and Tenses*, 1941.
OMAN, SIR CHARLES: *England Before the Norman Conquest*, 1938.
RYE, W. B.: *England as Seen by Foreigners in the Days of Elizabeth and James
    the First*, 1865.
STOW, JOHN: *Survey of London and Westminster*, 1598.
STUBBES, PHILIP: *Anatomie of Abuses*, 1583.
TAYLOR, JOHN: *Complaint of Christmas*, 1646.
THISTLETON-DYER, T. F.: *British Popular Customs*, 1891.
THOMS, WILLIAM J.: *Anecdotes and Traditions*, 1839.
TREVELYAN, G. M.: *English Social History*, 1944.
WILLIAMS, IOLO A.: *English Folk-Song and Dance*, 1935.
WILLIAMSON, GEORGE C.: *Curious Survivals*, 1923.
WOLSELEY, VISCOUNTESS: *The Countryman's Log-Book*, 1921.
WRIGHT, A. R. AND LONES, T. E.: *British Calendar Customs: England*, 3 Vols.,
    1936–8.

INDEX

INDEX

INDEX

ABOUT THE AUTHOR

Laurence Whistler was born in 1912.

He is perhaps best known today for his glass engraving, but was also a renowned poet and the author of many books, including *The English Festivals* and *The Initials in the Heart*.

In 1974 he was awarded the C.B.E. and in 2000, shortly before his death, a knighthood.